LF

Thomas Love Peacock

Twayne's English Authors Series

Herbert Sussman, Editor

Northeastern University

TEAS 456

THOMAS LOVE PEACOCK
(1785–1866)

Thomas Love Peacock

By James Mulvihill

University of Alberta

Twayne Publishers
A Division of G. K. Hall & Co. • *Boston*

To Abby

Thomas Love Peacock

James Mulvihill

Copyright 1987 by G.K. Hall & Co.
All rights reserved.
Published by Twayne Publishers
A Division of G.K. Hall & Co.
70 Lincoln Street
Boston, Massachusetts 02111

Copyediting supervised by Lewis DeSimone
Book production by Janet Zietowski
Book design by Barbara Anderson

Typeset in 11 pt. Garamond
by Modern Graphics, Inc., Weymouth, Massachusetts

Printed on permanent/durable acid-free paper
and bound in the United States of America

Library of Congress Cataloging in Publication Data

Mulvihill, James.
    Thomas Love Peacock.

    (Twayne's English authors series ; TEAS 456)
    Bibliography: p.
    Includes index.
    1. Peacock, Thomas Love, 1785–1866—Criticism and
interpretation.   I. Title.   II. Series.
PR5164.M85   1987   823'.7   87–15003
ISBN 0–8057–6957–9 (alk. paper)

Contents

About the Author
Preface
Acknowledgments
Chronology

Chapter One
The Laughing Philosopher   1

Chapter Two
Youth and Apprenticeship: The Poetry   12

Chapter Three
The Comic Spirit and *Headlong Hall*:
New Beginnings   26

Chapter Four
Melincourt and *Nightmare Abbey:*
Two Responses to Shelley   46

Chapter Five
Crotchet Castle and *Gryll Grange:*
The Mature Voice   69

Chapter Six
Maid Marian and *The Misfortunes of Elphin:*
Satiric Romance   92

Chapter Seven
Essays and Reviews: Peacock as Critic   110

Chapter Eight
Conclusion   121

Notes and References   127
Selected Bibliography   132
Index   136

About the Author

James Mulvihill received his Ph.D. from McMaster University in Hamilton, Canada, and is assistant professor of English at the University of Alberta. He has published articles in journals such as *SEL, Keats-Shelley Journal, English Studies,* and *Nineteenth-Century Fiction,* among others. Currently, he is working on a study of William Hazlitt.

Preface

The place of Thomas Love Peacock (1785–1866) in English literary history depends on a tiny, though highly characteristic, body of comic-satiric fiction. Indeed, Peacock's country-house settings and the collections of philosophers and cranks (not always mutually exclusive terms in Peacock) who inhabit them are so closely associated with his work as to be synonymous with the fictional quality often described as "Peacockian." Essentially, this "Peacockian" quality involves inordinate amounts of talk, sometimes absurd but always immensely learned, by characters who each embody a particular intellectual obsession. Talk is a crucial element, copious amounts of talk on a bewildering variety of subjects, for the hallmark of the Peacockian novel is an inexhaustible, exuberant eclecticism. Peacock's novels are in this sense novels of talk, their characters seeming to exist solely for the sake of what they have to say. And in the end it is the ideas that these characters utter that determine who they are, what they do, even what happens to them. Tensions and conflicts in a Peacock novel arise when these ideas clash, as they almost always seem to do.

Indeed, to have read one of the myriad debates on any of the myriad topics put forth in these novels is inevitably to ask: but where does *Peacock* stand on this? The answer is hardly ever clear-cut, and it is the rare reader who, at one time or another, has not agreed with James Spedding, who wrote in 1839 that Peacock "dwells more habitually among doubts and negations than we believe good for any man."[1] Spedding's reservations have been frequently repeated, and not always as tentatively, by modern critics like Mario Praz, Humphrey House, and A. E. Dyson, among others. The ideas that Peacock presents, according to Dyson, are merely part of the pageant:

They need, for Peacock's purpose, to be both simplified and arrested: simplified so that original notions sound wildly eccentric; and arrested so that one simplified idea can clash with its opposite to the greatest effect. The result falls short, one need scarcely add, of synthesis.[2]

Only recently has this view been definitively challenged and Peacock's fiction been regarded as more than an eccentric, and inconclusive, *potpourri* of undigested opinion. "He did write about key subjects at key times," insists Marilyn Butler, for example, "and with a degree of seriousness, and intelligence, that illuminates them still."[3]

Intended as a general introduction to Peacock, the present study takes as its premise this view that Peacock is to be taken seriously as both an artist and as an observer of his age—indeed, the two functions, in Peacock's case, are closely related. For this reason I have laid some emphasis on Peacock's notion of literary vocation, namely, his view of the writer as a responsive and sensitive gauge to his age, and, more specifically, simply as an engaged citizen. In a related connection, I am concerned to give a sense of the distinctiveness of each of Peacock's novels. Humphrey House expresses a common perception of first-time readers of Peacock when he complains that these novels "are all products of a single impulse and have very little separate artistic being."[4] The point, as I hope to show, is that the integrity of a Peacock novel depends not so much on organic artistic structure as on the particularity of its response to particular topical issues—"key subjects at key times."

To the small but dedicated corps of readers who have written about Peacock through the years I owe a debt that cannot be and, I fear, has not been, sufficiently repaid in my notes. I wish to thank Herbert Sussman, whose discerning, conscientious, and prompt editing made the process that produced this volume a pleasant one for me. Most of all I thank my wife Abby for her enthusiasm and concern.

James Mulvihill

University of Alberta

Acknowledgments

I wish to thank the editors of the following journals for their permission to use material originally published by them: © 1984 by the Keats-Shelley Association of America. Reprinted from *Keats-Shelley Journal* 33: 130–47; © 1983 by the Regents of the University of California. Reprinted from *Nineteenth-Century Fiction* 38, no. 3: 253–70, by permission of the Regents; © 1984 by Robert H. Canary and Henry Kozicki. Reprinted from *CLIO* 13, no. 3:227–46.

Chronology

1785   Born 18 October at Weymouth in Dorsetshire.

1788   Death of father (?); moves to Chertsey with mother to live with maternal grandparents.

1791–1799   Attends school at Englefield Green.

1800–1805?   Lives with mother in London; employed there as clerk.

1804   *The Monks of St. Mark.*

1806   *Palmyra and Other Poems.*

1808–1809   Works as personal secretary aboard H.M.S. *Venerable.*

1809   Resigns position on *Venerable;* embarks on expedition up Thames River to gather material for poem on Thames; during trip to Wales meets future wife Jane Gryffydh.

1810   *The Genius of the Thames.*

1811–1813   Writes two versified farces, *The Dilettanti* and *The Three Doctors.*

1812   *The Philosophy of Melancholy;* meets Shelley.

1813   *Sir Hornbook;* visits Shelleys at Bracknell, and tours Lake District and Scotland with them.

1814   *Sir Proteus.*

1815   Moves to village of Marlow, and continues association with Shelley in nearby Bishopsgate.

1816   *Headlong Hall*

1817   *Melincourt.*

1818   *Rhododaphne;* Shelleys leave England to settle in Italy; *Nightmare Abbey;* begins and leaves uncompleted "Essay on Fashionable Literature"; begins *Maid Marian.*

1819   Commences appointment at East India Company.

1820   Marries Jane Gryffyd; "Four Ages of Poetry."

1822   *Maid Marian.*

1826   Death of daughter Margaret; wife becomes permanent "nervous invalid."

1827–1839   Various reviews and essays in *Westminster Review,* the *Globe,* the *Examiner,* the *Edinburgh Review,* the *London Review,* and *Bentley's Miscellany.*

1829   *The Misfortunes of Elphin.*

1831   *Crotchet Castle.*

1833   Death of mother.

1837   *Paper Money Lyrics* (written during winter of 1825–1826).

1849   Daughter Mary Ellen marries George Meredith.

1851   Death of wife.

1856   Retires from East India Company.

1857   Death of daughter Rosa Jane; Mary Ellen leaves her husband, scandal ensues.

1859–1860   "Memoirs of Percy Bysshe Shelley."

1861   *Gryll Grange;* death of daughter Mary Ellen.

1866   Dies 23 January.

Chapter One

The Laughing Philosopher

"How far, we must ask ourselves, is a book influenced by its writer's life," asks Virginia Woolf, "how far is it safe to let the man interpret the writer?"[1] In the case of Thomas Love Peacock this question may seem to be beside the point, for in an age preoccupied with the lives of its writers, Peacock managed to lead a very private and, so far as his biographers are concerned, inaccessible life. Indeed, we know comparatively little about this life beyond its main outlines— the failed romantic poet turned satiric novelist, the friend of Shelley, the trusted and capable official of the East India Company, the old epicurean living in contented seclusion from a now unfamiliar world.

Peacock's views on the propriety of letting the man interpret the writer, moreover, seem consistent with his personal reticence. In the preface to a reprint edition of his novels in 1837 he writes: "All these little publications appeared originally without prefaces. I left them to speak for themselves; and I thought I might very fitly preserve my own impersonality, having never intruded on the personality of others, nor taken any liberties but with public conduct and public opinions."[2] While Peacock's claim that he has never dealt with private "personalities" is valid, it is also true that "personality" plays a crucial role in his satire nevertheless. According to Humphrey House, as a satirist Peacock "dealt . . . only with thought as it emerged into opinion or emotional attitude."[3] Despite the finally deprecating nature of this estimate, House puts his finger on an important aspect of Peacock's satire. If the personalities of Peacock's characters seem almost wholly based on the ideas expressed by these characters, the reverse also applies, for ideas in Peacock are conditioned by personality. And behind the clash of opinion— opinion colored by temperament—that characterizes the Peacockian novel, behind Peacock the novelist, is something of Peacock the man, elusive and seemingly contradictory, but comprehending in himself the multiplicity of opinions that are his characters and his character.

Childhood and Youth

Thomas Love Peacock was born on 18 October 1785 at Weymouth in Dorset, the only child of Samuel and Sarah Peacock (née Love). The father, Samuel, of whom little is known, seems to drop out of sight entirely, although a doubtful family tradition has it that he died in 1788. In this year Sarah left London with her son for the Thames village of Chertsey where her parents were living. Thenceforth, the dominant male influence in the child's life was the grandfather, Thomas Love, a former Master in the Royal Navy who was retired on half-pay after having been wounded in a naval action. Similar circumstances force the retirement of Captain Hawltaught in Peacock's second novel, *Melincourt,* and Thomas Love is thought to have provided the model for this minor fictional character. Certainly, it is tempting to trace Captain Hawltaught's taste for wine and rollicking catches, not to mention Peacock's own penchant for such things, to old Thomas.

The more lasting and significant parental influence, however, was the maternal one. Sarah Love Peacock seems to have been a remarkable woman. A widow in straitened circumstances following the death of her husband, she nevertheless encouraged young Thomas's studies and, herself a writer of verse, was likely a motivating force behind his literary aspirations. Indeed, until her death in 1833 Sarah was her son's most trusted critic, reading all his books before publication. According to Edith Nicolls, a granddaughter of Peacock: "There existed between Mrs. Peacock and her son Thomas the deepest love and sympathy; she was a woman of no common order of mind; he read all his writings to her, consulting her judgment, and seeking her criticisms; he often said that, after his mother's death, he wrote with no interest, as his heart was not in the work" (1:xix-xx). If a family tradition is correct, Peacock came by his ironic bent honestly, for Sarah's favorite author was reportedly the historian Gibbon, whose ironic view of man and society is not unlike that which underlies Peacock's fiction. It seems likely too that the energetic, independent heroines in the novels owe something to this spirited and intelligent woman, as do surely the elderly and engaging Misses Evergreen and Ilex of *Melincourt* and *Crotchet Castle* respectively. Except for a few brief intervals, Peacock and his mother never lived apart, and Sarah's death was felt keenly by her son. "I passed many of my best years with my mother," he remarked as an old man, "taking more pleasure in reading than in society" (1:xix).

We know relatively little about Peacock's childhood. A very handsome child, he is said to have once attracted the attention of Queen Charlotte so that she stopped her carriage to kiss him. Another anecdote, related by Peacock in an autobiographical essay entitled "The Abbey House," concerns a childhood friend named Charles:

Charles was fond of romances. The *Mysteries of Udolpho,* and all the ghost and goblin stories of the day, were his familiar reading. I cared little about them at that time; but he amused me by narrating their grimmest passages. He was very anxious that the Abbey House should be haunted; but it had no strange sights or sounds, and no plausible tradition to hang a ghost on (8:33–34).

On the one occasion Charles did actually seem to see a ghost, it turned out to be only a tall bunch of white flowers blown by the wind in the garden. "It was a cruel disappointment to Charles, who was obliged to abandon all hopes of having the house haunted," recalls Peacock (8:35). Although the incident is related from the perspective of middle age, perhaps something of the detachment and irony of the future author of *Nightmare Abbey* can be detected in the amusement with which the young Thomas here indulges his friend's fancies.

At the age of six Peacock was sent to the Englefield House School. The master at Englefield, John Harris Wicks, "was not much of a scholar," according to Peacock, but "had the art of inspiring his pupils with a love of learning" (8:259)—a love that Peacock, who despised those who spoke of "finishing" their education, would cultivate to the end of his life. Young Thomas was a precocious student, as his few surviving writings from this time indicate. According to a family tradition, Wicks had high hopes for the boy, predicting "that he would prove one of the most remarkable men of his day" (1:xxiii).

Peacock's formal education was brief, for he left Englefield before he was thirteen years of age to take up employment as a clerk in a London firm. He and his mother lived for some five or six years in London. During this time he competed successfully in an essay writing contest sponsored in 1800 by a children's magazine called the *Monthly Preceptor, or, Juvenile Library,* and in 1804 published privately a piece of light verse entitled *The Monks of St. Mark.* According to a doubtful family tradition, the young Peacock had access to the collections at the British Museum where, his granddaughter writes, "he devoted his whole time to reading the authors of ancient Greece and Rome, studying at the same time the architectural remains—the statues, bas reliefs, &c." (1:xxvi). What is certain is that Peacock maintained a strong interest in the classics, and seems somehow to have kept up his studies on his own, despite the demands of working life.

Little is known about Peacock's life during this period. His first volume of verse, *Palmyra and other Poems,* appeared in 1806, and in 1808 he began a year's service as a captain's clerk aboard the H.M.S. *Venerable.* Peacock seems not to have relished his time aboard the *Venerable,* which he characterized as a "floating inferno" (8:162), but he did manage to write some occasional verse during this year, and to begin an ambitious long poem entitled *The Genius of the Thames.* By the spring of 1809 he had resigned his posting on the *Venerable* and was taking a walking tour to the source of the Thames to gather additional material for his poem, which was published in 1810. A third volume of verse, *The Philosophy of Melancholy,* followed in 1812, and that same year Peacock met another young poet named Percy Bysshe Shelley.

Friendship with Shelley

It is probable that Peacock met Shelley in London through a mutual friend, Edward Hookham, the publisher and bookseller. A friendship did not develop until the following year, although Peacock, Shelley's senior, likely impressed the younger man with his learning and wide-ranging interests. Lists of books ordered by Shelley at this time contain titles undoubtedly suggested by Peacock from his own reading.

For his part, Peacock may have seen reflected in Shelley the extravagant attitudes and opinions he had himself been professing in the rather posturing, romantic verse he had been writing up to this point. In his memoirs of Shelley, written some half century later, Peacock insisted particularly on the young poet's tendency toward romantic self-dramatization, and he may have noted a similar tendency in his younger self. Certainly, Shelley's comments at this time regarding his new friend suggest a certain coolness and skeptical detachment on the part of Peacock: "His enthusiasm is not very ardent, nor his views very comprehensive: but he is neither superstitious, ill-tempered, dogmatical, or [*sic*] proud."[4] On the other hand, Peacock clearly saw more in Shelley than just a reflection of his own earlier flirtation with the sentimental-romantic. J. B. Priestley suggests that Shelley provided a "touchstone for genuine romantic feeling," forcing Peacock to acknowledge the falseness of his own romantic enthusiasms.[5] Both views are equally credible and each carries a germ of truth. Shelley appears in Peacock's fiction as both the idealized Mr. Forester of *Melincourt* and the absurd Scythrop Glowry of *Nightmare Abbey*.

Friendship with Shelley also introduced Peacock to a wider circle of acquaintance. In 1813 Peacock visited Shelley and Shelley's wife Harriet in Bracknell, where he came into contact with the social group that had gathered around the young poet and radical. The Boinvilles and the Newtons were the main members of this group of provincial dilettanti, who espoused heterodox opinions on a number of subjects, chiefly religion and politics. Constituted, according to Thomas Jefferson Hogg, a mutual friend, of "two or three sentimental young butchers, an eminently philosophical tinker, and several very unsophisticated medical practitioners,"[6] such a set must have appealed to Peacock's satiric instincts, as his later account of Bracknell suggests:

At Bracknell, Shelley was surrounded by a numerous society, all in a great measure of his own opinions in relation to religion and politics, and the larger portion of them in relation to the vegetable diet. But they wore their rue with a difference. Every one of them adopting some of the articles of the faith of their general church, had each nevertheless some predominant crotchet of his or her own, which left a number of open questions for earnest and not always temperate discussion. I was sometimes irreverent enough to laugh at the fervour with which opinions utterly unconducive to any practical result were battled for as matters of the highest importance to the well-being of mankind. (8:70)

This could be the sketch for a typical Peacock novel.

One Bracknell figure, in fact, J. F. Newton, would appear in several of Peacock's novels under various pseudonyms and seems to have been a prototypical Peacockian crotcheteer. Described by Pea-

cock as "the absolute impersonation of a single theory" (8:71),
Newton was a fanatical vegetarian who believed that all man's misfortunes, physical and moral, were due to the consumption of meat
and alcohol. This primitivistic theory he contrived somehow to
connect to a belief in the zodiac. "He saw the Zodiac in everything,"
recalls Peacock, even on one occasion in the four horseshoes depicted
on a public-house sign. Insisting on a zodiacal significance in the
number four, Newton leadingly asked the innkeeper why there were
in fact four horseshoes and was answered: "Why, sir, I suppose
because a horse has four legs." "He bounced out in great indignation," relates Peacock of Newton, "and as soon as I joined him, he
said to me, 'Did you ever see such a fool?' " (8:73). Nevertheless,
Peacock was interested enough in Newton's theories to base on them
a serious poem entitled "Ahrimanes," begun sometime after 1813
and left unfinished in 1815.

Peacock's mocking attitude did not go unnoticed by the fervent
inmates of Bracknell. Peacock recalls that he and Harriet Shelley,
who was always ready to laugh along with him, "both lost caste
with some of the more hot-headed of the party" for their levity
(8:71). One of these hot-headed people, Mrs. Newton, characterized
Peacock as a "cold scholar" who possessed "neither taste nor feeling."
"This Shelley will perceive sooner or later," she predicted, "for his
warm nature craves sympathy, and I am convinced he will not meet
with it in his new acquaintance" (1:1v). Such expectations were to
be disappointed, however, for the two acquaintances, so seemingly
different from each other, were soon to become close friends.

During October and November 1813 Peacock traveled to the
Lake District and Scotland with the Shelleys. The Lakes seem particularly to have impressed Peacock, who resolved to establish a
private school there in Westmorland. (This was just one of the shifts
the impecunious Peacock was considering, along with emigration
to America). Indeed, he went so far as to write a prospectus outlining
the school's curriculum, which, along with classical studies, would
include Italian, French, and English literature, "generally too much
neglected in the education of youth" (8:431). This educational scheme
would be realized in fiction, if not in fact, in the beautiful and
intelligent heroine of *Melincourt,* Anthelia, who has followed just
such a course of study, also among the mountains of Westmorland.
During this trip Shelley embarked on a course of classical studies

under Peacock, whom he described in a letter as "a very mild, agreeable man, and a good scholar."[7]

In 1814 Shelley abandoned his wife Harriet to elope with Mary Godwin, a daughter of the political philosopher William Godwin and the feminist Mary Wollstonecraft. Peacock's sympathies were with the unfortunate Harriet, who committed suicide two years later. Relations between the two friends were evidently strained by the elopement, judging by references to Peacock in Shelley's letters, written from the Continent where he and Mary had fled, as "inconsiderate & cold."[8]

The eloped couple returned to England in the fall of 1814, and Peacock and Shelley were soon reconciled. With Mary Godwin, eventually Mary Shelley, Peacock was never on easy terms, although he appreciated that she was better suited to Shelley intellectually than poor Harriet had been. Ironically, it is due to Mary that we have at least a sketchy record of the developing friendship between the two young writers, for grudging entries in her journal record frequent visits to the Shelley household by Peacock. Indeed, by 1815 Peacock was living in a village named Marlow within walking distance of the Shelleys, who now lived in Bishopsgate and the following year moved to Marlow.

The years 1815 to 1818 were a productive period for both Peacock and Shelley and a time of close cooperation, if not of actual collaboration. Hogg, a member of this Marlow circle, called the winter of 1815–16, "a mere Atticism" (8:99), referring to their continuing classical studies. During this time Shelley wrote *Alastor* (1816), the title of which Peacock suggested, and *The Revolt of Islam* (1817), which Peacock helped to revise extensively for publication. Peacock wrote his first two novels, *Headlong Hall* (1816) and *Melincourt* (1817). Both these works evince the influence of his friendship with Shelley, from the debates on progress in *Headlong Hall* to the overtly liberal agenda of *Melincourt,* which clearly bears Shelley's imprint. Peacock also wrote his last long poem, *Rhododaphne* (1818), during this period.

In early 1818 the Shelleys sailed to Italy. Peacock, "lonely as a cloud, and as melancholy as a gib cat," as he told Hogg,[9] remained in Marlow, where he wrote his third novel, *Nightmare Abbey* (1818). He and Shelley corresponded regularly, Peacock keeping his friend abreast of political developments at home and sending packets of books, Shelley giving a sometimes lively and sometimes sorrowful commentary on his new life in Italy. In a verse-letter written to Maria Gisborne in 1820, a homesick Shelley remembered his friends back in England, among them "cameleopard" Peacock, whose "fine wit / Makes such a wound, the knife is lost in it."[10] The two friends were never to see each other again, for in July 1822 Shelley drowned in a sailing accident off the Italian coast.

The India House

In 1819 Peacock began an appointment in the Examiner's Office of the East India Company, where he would remain employed for the next three and a half decades. His duties for the company varied, but essentially the Examiner's department was in charge of coping with the vast number of reports and studies received every year from the company's Indian concerns. Indeed, when Peacock was hired, the company correspondence had fallen seriously into arrears, and the appointment called for a "higher than ordinary standard of qualifications" (1:xciv).

Peacock's career with the East India Company was a distinguished one. He became Chief Examiner in 1836 and held that post until his retirement in 1856. He spoke before parliamentary committees on various matters, and was instrumental in urging the East India Company's adoption of steam navigation. In this latter connection, indeed, he oversaw the construction of the company's first two steamships—calling them his "iron chickens." Duties at the India House also brought Peacock into a circle that included prominent utilitarian thinkers like James Mill, whom Peacock succeeded as Chief Examiner, and Mill's son, John Stuart Mill, who eventually succeeded Peacock in that post. Acquaintance with the Mills seems to have led to an introduction to the father of English utilitarianism, Jeremy Bentham, with whom Peacock dined often for several years.

Utilitarianism is a particularly rational philosophy, which places a supreme value on "utility"—i.e., whatever promotes "the greatest happiness of the greatest numbers" in society—subordinating everything else, such as aesthetics and conventional morality, to that principle. Thus it seems a curious circumstance that Peacock, in his novels the satiric scourge of just such exclusive intellectual

systems as utilitarianism, should have found himself among such a
circle of acquaintance. An anecdote related by a friend in 1853,
however, indicates that Peacock retained the clear-sighted irony that
distinguishes his satire. Bentham, true to his utilitarian precepts,
had directed in his will that his body be dissected following his
death; James Mill, who was evidently present at the dissection—
to pay his last respects, no doubt—excitedly told Peacock that
Bentham's brain had exuded an oil which was unfreezable and which
might prove useful for the oiling of chronometers in high latitudes:

"The less you say about that, Mill" said Peacock, "the better it will be
for *you;* because if the fact once becomes known, just as we see now in
the newspapers advertisements to the effect that a fine bear is to be killed
for his grease, we shall be having advertisements to the effect that a fine
philosopher is to be killed for his oil" (1:clxxv).

Indeed, utilitarians, political economists, and the like are often
satirized in Peacock's works of this period.

Employment with the East India Company also brought financial
security. For the first time Peacock could seriously consider marrying
and settling down to raise a family. In November 1819 he wrote a
rather formal letter to one Jane Gryffydh, whom he had met in
1809 during a stay in Wales, proposing marriage. Although she
had neither seen nor heard from Peacock for eight years, Jane replied
within the month, and the two were married in March of the
following year in Wales. A first child, Mary Ellen, was born in
1821, followed by three others over the next five years. The couple
took a house at Lower-Halliford on the Thames, which would remain
Peacock's home to the end of his life. Married happiness for Peacock
was short-lived, however, for with the sudden death in 1826 of
their second-born, a girl named Margaret Love, Jane suffered a
breakdown, and for the rest of her life was a "nervous invalid."
Peacock's mother assumed the household duties at Halliford until
her death in 1833.

Responsibilities at the India House still left Peacock time for
some writing, however. *Maid Marian,* begun in 1818, was completed in 1821 and published the following year. *The Misfortunes of
Elphin* appeared in 1829, and *Crotchet Castle* two years later in 1831.
Peacock also wrote some occasional verse, most notably a collection
of satiric poems entitled *Paper Money Lyrics,* written during the

winter of 1825–26, but not published until 1837. In 1820 Peacock had published his famous essay "The Four Ages of Poetry" in *Olliers' Literary Miscellany,* and for the next two decades produced a number of essays and reviews for periodicals such as the *Westminster Review,* the *London Review, Bentley's Miscellany* (under the editorship of Charles Dickens), and the *Edinburgh Review,* as well as a substantial body of musical criticism for the *Globe* and the *Examiner.* From 1839 to 1850 Peacock seems not have published anything; however, in the 1850s he contributed a few pieces to *Fraser's Magazine.* All the while, he commuted between Halliford and the India House in London.

Retirement and Old Age

When he retired from the East India Company in 1856, Peacock could look back with satisfaction on a successful career as an administrator and cherish a minor but respectable literary reputation. His personal life had not been free from tragedy. His wife died in 1851 after nearly twenty-five years as a permanent invalid; surely even more trying for him was the unhappy marriage of his favorite daughter Mary Ellen to the novelist George Meredith. Married in 1849, the couple led a dreary and impecunious existence that only served to exacerbate their lack of compatibility. In 1857 Mary Ellen deserted Meredith and left the country with the painter Henry Wallis. She returned alone to England in 1859, dying two years later in 1861, abandoned and disgraced. Although he did not attend the funeral, Peacock is said to have been with his daughter in her last illness.[11]

Peacock was surprisingly prolific in his retirement. After a full thirty years of silence as a novelist, he wrote *Gryll Grange* (1861), as well as starting and abandoning several other works of fiction at this time. The years 1859 and 1860 saw the publication in *Fraser's Magazine* of his "Memoirs of Percy Bysshe Shelley." His final years, however, spent in almost complete seclusion, Peacock devoted mainly to reading. One of his infrequent visitors observed that "age had mellowed and subdued the 'cameo-leopard [*sic*],' but the 'fine wit,' as I very speedily discovered, was as keen as ever."[12] Peacock died peacefully in 1866 at the age of eighty-one. An obituary notice in the *Athenaeum* remembered him as a satirist who exhibited "the philosophies and paradoxes of the time with an epigrammatic keenness, and withal a genial recognition of all that is best, highest, and most liberal" (1:ccx).

Chapter Two

Youth and Apprenticeship: The Poetry

"The Four Ages of Poetry" is commonly viewed as Peacock's definitive estimate of contemporary poetry, including his own. This essay traces poetry's decline from primitive vigor (the ages of iron and gold) through the polished classical verse of the Augustan silver age to, finally, the artificial primitivism of the brass age, as Peacock terms his own age. Peacock's poetry straddles the silver and brass ages, as did much minor verse of the period.[1] Its forms are Augustan, the ode, the elegy, the topographical poem, while its mood and subject-matter are romantic. It is, essentially, the poetry of a previous generation—poets of the mid-eighteenth century like Thomas Gray, William Collins, James Thompson, Thomas and Joseph Warton, and John Dyer, who anticipated the romantic poets of the early nineteenth century—and its conventions show signs of wear. Melancholy, solitude, and nostalgia for things past are among its chief elements. Abstract personifications and lofty moralizing abound. Its diction is stiff and declamatory, employing hyphenated phrases and conventional epithets. J. B. Priestley aptly sums up these qualities in the following pastiche:

As usual, the poet with his *lay* and his *numbers, roves* through *smiling plains, o'er mountains dreary,* on *desolate shores,* or *lightly springs* to meet some *matchless nymph* in some *fair bower,* attended by the *sylvan muses* and the *genial rays* of the sun, and his *thoughts are beguil'd* by *visions wild* because he is *creative Fancy's child,* and at once the victim of *dark Despair* and the pupil of *inspiring Hope.*[2]

Rarely more than competent as a poet, Peacock also had the disadvantage of writing at the end of an exhausted tradition.

The fact remains, however, that Peacock turned to fiction only after devoting much of his early manhood to becoming a poet. During that time he produced several volumes of poetry—*Palmyra and other Poems* (1806), *The Genius of the Thames* (1810), *The Philosophy of Melancholy* (1812), and *Rhododaphne: or the Thessalian Spell* (1818)—as well as a fair body of miscellaneous verse. Indeed, he was thirty when he wrote *Headlong Hall* (1816), the first of those eccentric satiric fictions on which his fame now rests. This seemingly abrupt shift in direction has been explained variously, but in reality it was not the clean break that a chronology of Peacock's works might suggest. The sensibility that informs the poetry is present in the fiction, although it is necessarily altered in emphasis. It might even be said that some of those very elements that often render Peacock's poetry stale—the nostalgia for a distant and improbable past, for instance—seem vital in the novels. More important, we can trace a development through the poetry, in both attitude and treatment, that looks forward to the fiction.

Palmyra and other Poems (1806)

The Palmyra volume marks Peacock's debut as a poet. His efforts prior to this are negligible except as they anticipate later tendencies. They include verse-letters written from school and experiments with different verse types: acrostics, epigrams, imitations, and the like. In 1800, while working as a clerk in London, the fifteen-year-old Peacock competed successfully for a prize offered by a children's magazine called the *Monthly Preceptor*. The subject was "Is History or Biography the more Improving Study?" Peacock's verse-essay, which solemnly pleads in favor of history, was praised by the *Preceptor* editors "not as a specimen of poetry particularly excellent, but as an extraordinary effort of genius in a boy of this age."[3] (Another prize was awarded to "Master Leigh Hunt, aged 15, educated at Christ's Hospital.") A second published work, *The Monks of St. Mark,* issued privately in 1804, is an early indication of Peacock's penchant for boisterous slapstick. It depicts the vinous antics of some cloister brothers who, when the poem's rollicking anapests have run their course, are "shortly all under the table together" (7:192).

Such high spirits are notably absent from *Palmyra and other Poems.* The title piece is an elegiac ode upon the ruins of Palmyra, a Syrian city identified with the Tadmor of the Old Testament. Peacock's inspiration for *Palmyra* was entirely literary. His main source was Robert Wood's *Ruins of Palmyra, otherwise Tedmore, in the desert*

(1753), from which he manufactured many of the explanatory notes included at the end of the poem, along with other extracts from Gibbon, Volney, Ossian, and the Book of Isaiah. The ruins-of-time theme is familiar enough in poetry; indeed, as Carl Dawson points out, James Grainger had already written his *Ode to Solitude, Palmyra, and Tedmore* in 1755.[4] During the 1830s Palmyra was still turning up as a subject for university prize poems.[5]

In *The Misfortunes of Elphin* Peacock would describe the picturesque tourist who "works himself up into a soliloquy of philosophical pathos, on the vicissitudes of empire and the mutability of all sublunary things, interrupted only by an occasional peep at his watch" (4:101). No humorous deprecation relieves this mood in *Palmyra:*

> Yes, all are flown!
> I stand alone,
> At ev'ning's calm and pensive hour,
> Mid wasted domes,
> And mould'ring tombs,
> The wrecks of vanity and pow'r.
>   (6:13)

The opening stanzas dwell upon the desolation of the scene, evoking images of "blasted plain" and "pomp of ruin," all palely tinted by "sun's declining beam" (6:8–9). A historical account of the city's subjection and final destruction follows, complete with "Wild Confusion's fev'rish glare, / Horror, Madness, and Despair!" (6:16). The poem closes with reflections on the transitory nature of man's life on earth: "The varying deeds that mark the present time / Will be but shadows of the days gone by" (6:19). Conventional personifications stalk through the poem: Contemplation with "downcast eye," Love, Stern Despair, Black Revenge, Fear and Hope, and of course Time, with "scythe, and sand." In theme, mood, and diction—in every respect—*Palmyra* is formal and academic verse. Shelley's praise for *Palmyra* as "the finest piece of poetry I ever read"[6] is inexplicable.

Among the twenty or so shorter pieces accompanying this poem are miscellaneous lyrics, a group of satiric poems entitled "Nugae," and several Ossianic poems. In 1762 James Macpherson had published what purported to be a translation of a primitive epic by the

Gaelic poet Ossian. The poem was mainly fraudulent, but the literary vogue that grew around it was still current in Peacock's youth. Of the three Ossianic poems in the *Palmyra* volume, two, "Clonar and Tlamin" and "Foldath in the Cavern of Moma," are brief imitations, while "Fiolfar, King of Norway" is an extended narrative in the Ossianic mode.

Though Peacock would complain that *Palmyra* was *"strangled in its birth"* (8:188), the volume was well received by the reviewers. The *Poetical Register* thought Peacock "an author of very promising talents" (1:xxxiv), while the *Monthly Review* was sure that he had managed "to get a sip from the sacred fountain" (1:xxxiv). The *Critical Review* provided perhaps the clearest indication of the conservative standards by which *Palmyra* was being judged, for it approvingly detected "the fire of Gray" in Peacock's verse (1:xxxiv). The main interest of *Palmyra and other Poems* lies finally in what it tells us about Peacock's sensitivity to literary fashions, a trait that would be used to more effective purpose in the later satire.

The Genius of the Thames (1810)

During the years immediately following *Palmyra,* Peacock wrote little. In 1808 family connections secured him a post as under secretary to a naval commander, and he found himself aboard the H.M.S. *Venerable* complaining in letters to his publisher friend, Edward Hookham, that "as to writing poetry, or doing anything else that is rational, in this floating Inferno, it is almost next to a moral impossibility" (8:162). In fact, he did manage three prologues and an epilogue, written for dramatic performances on the ship, and a poem, "Stanzas Written at Sea," published in 1810. The "foam-crested billows" and "vast-rolling glory" of the latter piece notwithstanding, the *Venerable* never left harbor during Peacock's time aboard her. By March 1809 he had also completed the first draft of a poem about the Thames, which he sent to Hookham for consideration.

Unlike the subject of *Palmyra,* the Thames River was something of which Peacock had firsthand knowledge. He would live most of his life beside it or in its vicinity, and his associations with the surrounding countryside were genuine. Some traces of these personal associations may be detected in the finished work, but tradition has by far the more dominant presence. When submitting his first draft to Hookham, Peacock discovered his negligence "in omitting to mention, in the accompanying poem, Runnymead and Cowper's [*sic*] Hill" (8:166) and he promptly remedied the omission. In any case, the completed *Genius of the Thames* more than pays homage to tradition.

In his "Life of Denham" Samuel Johnson describes Sir John Denham's most famous work, *Cooper's Hill* (1655), as "a species of composition that may be denominated *local poetry,* of which the fundamental subject is some particular landscape, to be poetically described, with the addition of such embellishments as may be supplied by historical retrospection, or incidental meditation."[7] Denham's poem is credited with establishing the tradition of "local" or "topographical" poetry in English literature, celebrating hills, rivers, caves, and other such aspects of the landscape, a tradition which included Alexander Pope, John Dyer, and even William Wordsworth, as well as a host of minor poets. *Cooper's Hill* does not contain much specific description of scenery; it is more concerned with the historical associations of the places it describes, presenting copious extracts from British history overlaid with sundry moral observations. In his imitation of Denham's poem, *Windsor Forest* (1713), Pope provides much the same fare with an added measure of patriotism—"Earth's distant Ends our Glory shall behold"—and a mythological episode. Dyer's *Grongar Hill* (1726) contains less general moralizing and more specific scenery, but it is in Wordsworth's "Tintern Abbey" (1798) that nature becomes something more than a picturesque setting. Wordsworth infuses the particular locality described in his poem with an element of personal emotion that definitively sets "Tintern Abbey" off from its predecessors.

The Genius of the Thames is squarely in the earlier tradition of topographical poetry. The new style of poetry heralded by "Tintern Abbey" might not have existed for all the influence it seems to have had on Peacock's poem. "To thee I pour the votive lay, / Oh Genius of the silver Thames!" (6:111) cries the poet, but he is really addressing hidebound literary tradition. A catalog of rivers opens part 1. Yarrow, Tweed, Avon, Severn, Wye, and Dee are invoked, "but all, oh Thames! submit to thee, / The monarch-stream of Albion's isle" (6:113). Volga, Danube, Seine, Tiber, and Nile, among others, similarly submit to the Thames's sway. This patriotic strain is carried over to a section that reads much like a versified *Wealth of Nations:*

> Throned in Augusta's ample port,
> Imperial commerce holds her court,
> And Britain's power sublimes:
> To her the breath of every breeze
> Conveys the wealth of subject seas,
> And tributary climes.
>
> (6:118)

Indeed, although he admired the poem, Shelley was critical of its assumption "that commerce is prosperity."[8]

Perhaps Peacock sought to balance his paean to progress with the episode that closes part 1. Set in Britain's "eldest time," the episode relates how a young Roman legionnaire, wandering in a forest at night, chances upon a primitive rite being performed by an old Druid: "Sensations, wild and undefined, / Rushed on the Roman warrior's mind" (6:122–23). Thus "polished" civilized man confronts rude, primitive man; through the eyes of the bewildered Roman youth the modern reader is meant to marvel at the spectacle of untamed, primitive passion embodied in the old Druid. Peacock's point here—later elaborated into a habitual satiric stance—is surely that with the advance of civilization we have gained something and lost something. At the episode's end the Roman has mortally wounded the Druid, whose death song recalls at once Ossian and "Rule Britannia."

Part 2 is essentially a guided tour along the course of the Thames with literary and historical commentary. An extract from Peacock's own prefatory summary gives a good idea of this section: "Godstow nunnery: Rosamond. Oxford. Apostrophe to science. Nuneham Courtnay: Mason. The vale of Marlow. Hedsor. Cliefden. Windsor. Cooper's Hill. Runnymead. Twitnam: Pope. Richmond: Thompson." (6:132), and so forth. The poem concludes with reflections on the fall of nations. *Palmyra* has not been left far behind.

When *The Genius of the Thames* appeared, the *Satirist* published a hostile review, which complained that "the composition leaves no distinct impression on the mind" (1:xli). The *British Critic,* the *Antijacobin Review,* and the *Monthly Review,* however, were more favorable. "A composition which on the whole is so good that it deserves to be better," was the *Monthly Review*'s judgment (1:xli). The poem's interest today is mainly historical. The explanatory notes appended to it tell us much about what Peacock was reading at this time, and letters written to Hookham during the period of its composition provide insight into Peacock's development as a writer. In one of these letters, during the course of his Thames expedition, Peacock reflects that "the Thames is almost as good a subject for a satire as a panegyric"—and he goes on to imagine how a satirist, as opposed to a panegyrist, might treat the subject (8:172–73). There is some hint here of things to come, although, as always in Peacock's poetry, the more conventional voice would prevail for a time. "The problem," as Marilyn Butler observes, "was to find a form capable of expressing what were really more equivocal attitudes."[9]

The Philosophy of Melancholy

In January 1810 Peacock undertook an expedition to North Wales, where he was captivated by the mountains and waterfalls of Merionethshire. The beautiful Welsh countryside, described in letters to Hookham, would appear later in Peacock's fiction, but it provided more immediate inspiration as well. Peacock spent some fifteen months in Merionethshire, wandering through its mountainous vales and reading the numerous books he requested from Hookham. He met his future wife, Jane Gryffyd, here and he must have felt a pang upon returning alone to England in April 1811. The remainder of this year was spent working on a new poem, *The Philosophy of Melancholy*.

In one of his letters to Hookham, written while still in Wales, Peacock claims a tendency toward melancholy:

You saw this exemplified in me last summer when I was sometimes skipping about the room, singing, and playing all sorts of ridiculous antics, at others doling out staves of sorrow, and meditating on daggers and laurel water. Such is the disposition of all votaries of the muses.

Indeed, "a certain degree of *noncomposity* is essential to the poetical character," he decides (8:183–84). Here, as in the poem Peacock was soon to write on the subject, however, emphasis should be placed on melancholy as a literary quality rather than as a personal attribute. An excerpt from another letter of this same period is probably more indicative of Peacock's real temperament: "On the the top of Cadair Idris, I felt how happy a man may be with a little money and a sane intellect, and reflected with astonishment and pity on the madness of the multitude" (8:191). Still, at points in *The Philosophy of Melancholy* we glimpse something of the poet, for in this work, more than in any of those preceding it, Peacock is drawing on personal experience. It is likely, for example, that the "fair form" praised in part 3—"now too far removed!"—refers to Jane Gryffyd. Part 1 concludes with a description of the mountain scenery of Merionethshire, which corresponds closely to similar descriptions in letters to Hookham. Moreover, references to a note of "retrospective attachment" underlying the poem recall Wordsworth's famous definition of poetry as "emotion recollected in tranquillity."[10] In a summary of part 3 Peacock describes the "feelings excited by revisiting scenes, and observing objects, which recall to us the intercourse of the friends whom we have loved and lost" (6:208).

Nevertheless, *The Philosophy of Melancholy* is cast largely in a traditional mold. It is descended from a long line of eighteenth-century descriptive pieces modeled loosely on "Il Penseroso," and invoking Melancholy, Despair, and any number of other abstract qualities. Indeed, Milton's poem rears its cowled head in part 1:

> Why loves the muse the melancholy lay?
> Why joys the bard, in autumn's closing day,
> To watch the yellow leaves, that round him sail,
> And hear a spirit moan in every gale?
> To seek, beneath the moon, at midnight hour,
> The ivied abbey, and the mouldering tower.
>
> (6:190)

The four sections of the poem enumerate the consolations of melancholy in every aspect of human life. It is melancholy, argues part 1, that allows the philosopher to endure life's vicissitudes: "No sudden change thy pensive votaries feel: / They mark the whirl of fortune's restless wheel / Taught by the past the coming hour to scan" (6:191). Similarly, part 2 continues, "Thy genial sway / The sister arts, a pensive train, obey" (6:199), and examples are cited from painting, music, and poetry. Part 3 deals with the beneficial influence of melancholy on the social affections, while in part 4 it is through melancholy that we rise to a philosophical acceptance of imperfection in the universe, and ascend even further "to the knowledge of that all-perfect wisdom, which arranges the whole in harmony" (6:186).

Although the *Eclectic Review* criticized the poem for "showy finery and sweet pretty nonsense,"[11] the verse in *The Philosophy of Melancholy* shows an improvement over earlier efforts. But it is not as a measure of its author's continuing poetic development that the poem is finally significant. *Palmyra* and *The Genius of the Thames* are traditional not only in form but in attitude: *Palmyra* ends on a note of Christian consolation, and *The Genius of the Thames* is nothing if not orthodox in its views on commerce and the British Empire. While still traditional in form, *The Philosophy of Melancholy* strikes a somewhat new note in terms of attitude. The poem concludes with a hymn to the all-powerful deity who is the principle of universal harmony— "One power, one spirit"—but Peacock's notes suggest that this is not necessarily the Christian god (6:245–46). A shorter poem also included in the volume, "The Spirit of Fire: a Mythological Ode," may only indicate a scholarly interest in other religious systems. It is noteworthy, however, that in a revised version of *Palmyra,* published the same year, the concluding Christian stanzas have been dropped and replaced with reflections on "Necessity's mysterious sway" (6:175). The heterodox friend of Shelley is finding his voice.

Rhododaphne: or the Thessalian Spell (1818)

The Philosophy of Melancholy signals the end of Peacock's first phase as a writer. Six years would pass before he attempted another long poem, and this would be his last. *Rhododaphne* bears the imprint of those intervening six years. In 1812 Peacock met Shelley, and the resulting friendship would prove influential for both writers. Indeed, Peacock's first three novels grew out of the constant interchange of ideas and views that occurred between the two friends during this period. During the summer and autumn of 1817 Shelley wrote *Laon and Cythna* (later *The Revolt of Islam),* and Peacock his last major poem, *Rhododaphne: or the Thessalian Spell,* which appeared the following year.

Shelley described *Rhododaphne* as "a story of classical mystery and magic—the transfused essence of Lucian, Petronius, and Apuleius."[12] While there is nothing in it of the satiric import of these latter authors, the poem has an air of authenticity that may have suggested the parallel to Shelley. Voluminously read in classical literature (he was nicknamed "Greeky-Peeky" by a friend), Peacock was as familiar with ancient Greece as he was with North Wales or the Thames valley—perhaps more so, in some ways, for the setting of his Greek romance seems more completely realized than those of the earlier works. In *Rhododaphne* Peacock was dealing with a subject that genuinely interested him and that would continue to interest him deeply throughout his life. In his ficiton it is ancient Greece, particularly republican Athens, that most often serves as satiric norm, the ideal of civilized society. Other young writers of the period too were looking back to ancient Greece, among them John Keats, who was writing *Endymion* (1818) at the same time that Peacock was writing *Rhododaphne*. Although Peacock criticized *Endymion* for its inaccuracies, that poem and the later *Lamia* (1820) share a common inspiration with Peacock's poem.

Unlike the earlier works, *Rhododaphne* is a narrative poem. Anthemion, a young shepherd from Arcadia, travels to the Temple of Love at Thespia in order to pray for the recovery of his beloved, Calliroë, who is dying of a mysterious illness. Here he meets a beautiful enchantress named Rhododaphne who falls in love with him. Warned by an elderly sage that Rhododaphne is evil, Anthemion is nevertheless unable to resist her magic. She kisses him, exulting:

> "These lips are mine; the spells have won them,
> Which round and round thy soul I twine;
> And be the kiss I print upon them
> Poison to all lips but mine!"
>
> (7:38–39)

The young shepherd returns to Arcadia and finds Calliroë well, but when he rashly kisses her, she appears to die, poisoned by his kiss. Anthemion becomes a guilty wanderer, roaming aimlessly "oe'r plain and steep" (7:49), until, kidnapped by pirates, he discovers a beautiful fellow captive to be none other than Rhododaphne. Through the latter's magic, the two are shipwrecked together, and Anthemion soon finds himself set up in a splendid palace—actually a humble cottage magically transformed—living with his lovely enchantress. Though won over by Rhododaphne's wiles, Anthemion is unable to forget his dead sweetheart. The story reaches its climax when Urania (heavenly or spiritual love) kills Rhododaphne, breaking the spell that has kept Calliroë in a death-like trance. Reunited with Anthemion, Calliroë forgives the unfortunate Rhododaphne: " 'Twas for Anthemion's love she erred!" (7:88).

As narrative poetry, *Rhododaphne* is an excellent specimen of its kind. To say the poem is readable is not to damn with faint praise, for this is a quality absent from much of the period's enormous body of narrative verse. Its similarities with *Lamia* are obvious: the puritanical old sage, the magic palace, the enchantress destroyed for her erring infatuation. Perhaps too the pictorial quality of its verse, something lacking in Peacock's earlier poems, is similarly Keatsian:

> He bore a simple wild-flower wreath
> Narcissus, and the sweet-briar rose;
> Vervain, and flexile thyme, that breathe
> Rich fragrance; modest heath, that glows
> With purple bells; the amaranthe bright,
> That no decay nor fading knows,
>
> (7:12)

as is its sensuousness, also unusual in Peacock,

> His eyes swim
> With dizziness. The lamps grow dim,
> And tremble, and expire. No more.
> Darkness is there, and Mystery:
> And Silence keeps the golden key
> Of Beauty's bridal door.
>
> (7:75)

Peacock's last long poem, *Rhododaphne* is in some ways his most genuinely romantic.

The reviews were favorable, although the *Literary Gazette* strangely insisted on the uniqueness of *Rhododaphne*'s Greek subject: "Leaving our Scotts, Southeys, Byrons, Moores, Campbells, Wordsworths, this reverts to classic ground" (1:lxxviii). Byron, for one, said he would have been glad "to father the Grecian enchantress himself" (1:lxxviii), and indeed Peacock was responding to what was a very current enthusiasm in his generation. Moreover, republican Athens had long occupied a place in liberal political symbolism, and certainly the Hellenic interests of Shelley and Peacock, and of other young liberals, had radical overtones, extending into areas of morality and religion, as well as of political reform. While it may seem extreme to see in *Rhododaphne,* as Marilyn Butler does, "an assault on Christian sexual ethics,"[13] Peacock's habitual religious heterodoxy, hardly tempered by association with Shelley, lends strength to this view. Butler argues that Anthemion and Rhododaphne are victims of repressive sexual taboos—the very taboos, presumably, that forced Shelley (with Peacock's help) to excise sensitive passages from *Laon and Cythna*—which are merely the personal counterpart of more political forms of repression. In any case, it is clear from *Rhododaphne* that Peacock looked for his ideal of civilization to the ancient Greeks: "Shunning the living world, I dwell, and hear, / Reverent, the creeds they held, the tales they told" (7:8). As a confession of faith, these lines would prove enduring.

Miscellaneous Poetry

Peacock wrote and published other poetry, of course, particularly in the years between *The Philosophy of Melancholy* and *Rhododaphne.* Two plays written during the period, *The Dilettanti* (1812?) and *The Three Doctors* (1813), are versified farces, which, with their country-house settings and crotchety characters, clearly prefigure the novels, albeit crudely. In their excessive slapstick they look back to the juvenile *Monks of St. Mark.* Another work, *Sir Hornbook* (1814), is more interesting in some ways. Described on its title page as a "Grammatico-Allegorical Ballad," it is a short children's grammar that surveys the parts of speech by representing them as figures from chivalric romance. Hence its hero, Sir Hornbook, whose merry men number "full six and twenty"—"The first that came was mighty A, / the last was little Z" (6:264). *The Round Table; or King Arthur's Feast* (1817) is also a children's work, this time surveying the kings of England.

Some other pieces written at this time anticipate, in different ways, later preoccupations in the satire. *Ahrimanes,* begun some time after 1813 and never completed, was to have been an epic treatment of the opposition between good and evil. Based on the ancient Zoroastrian mythology, it is strongly influenced by the ideas of Peacock's Bracknell acquaintance J.F. Newton, who would serve as the original for several caricatures in the novels. Moreover, Peacock's eclectic and out-of-the-way background reading for this poem, including works by authors like Lord Monboddo and Sir William

Drummond, would provide the material for a good deal of the novels' satire as well. Shelley drew on the fragmentary *Ahrimanes* for the Zoroastrianism of *Laon and Cythna*.

Sir Proteus: a Satirical Ballad (1814) would seem to be even more prophetic of things to come. Not only is its subject the Lake Poets, who appear often in the novels, but its treatment of them is explicitly satiric—although perhaps it is closer to being invective. Lacking the mock-epic sweep of Byron's *Vision of Judgement* (1822), *Sir Proteus* is likewise an attack on Robert Southey, who had been made Poet Laureate the preceding year. Peacock's line in this work is that of liberal radicals at the time, castigating Southey and his fellow Lake Poets, Coleridge and Wordsworth, for deserting their former republican ideals and selling out to the Established Powers. Unfortunately, the satire is often obscure and freighted down with numerous notes. Peacock's only other extended attempt at satiric verse is a series of short poems entitled *Paper Money Lyrics,* written in 1825–26 but not published until 1837. The target of his satire here is "that arch class of quacks, who call themselves political economists" (7:99), and in particular the "Scotch Economists," who come in for frequent drubbings in the novels as well.

After *Rhododaphne* Peacock committed himself to prose, but still wrote occasional verse, scattering throughout his novels numerous songs and ballads. Indeed, these brief snatches of verse are a distinguishing mark of his fiction, whether convivial,

> A heeltap! a heeltap! I never could bear it!
> So fill me a bumper, a bumper of claret!
> Let the bottle pass freely, don't shirk it not [*sic*] spare it,
> For a heeltap! a heeltap! I never could bear it!
> > (*Headlong Hall,* 1:57),

or sentimental,

> I played with you 'mid cowslips blowing,
> When I was six and you were four;
> When garlands weaving, flower-balls throwing,
> Were pleasures soon to please no more.
> Through groves and meads, o'er grass and heather,
> With little playmates, to and fro,
> We wandered hand in hand together;

> But that was sixty years ago.
>
> *(Gryll Grange,* 5:146)

In the latter strain too (although not included in a novel) is a brief personal lyric entitled "Newark Abbey," written in 1842. Admired by Tennyson, this little poem grew out of Peacock's memories of his first love:

> I gaze, where August's sunbeam falls
> Along these grey and lonely walls,
> Till in its light absorbed appears
> The lapse of five-and-thirty years.
>
> (7:252)

It has been aptly said that Peacock achieved poetry only when he ceased to be a poet.

Peacock courted the muse for some fifteen years and thus must be regarded as more than desultory in his poetic efforts. But he was composing verse at a time when genuine poetry was being created. Shelley's private estimate of his friend as a "nursling of the exact and superficial school in poetry"[14] is hard but just. Peacock's talents, as Shelley well knew, lay elsewhere.

Chapter Three
The Comic Spirit and
Headlong Hall:
New Beginnings

In 1816, when he published *Headlong Hall,* Peacock became a novelist. Although he would continue to compose verse, writing *Rhododaphne* in 1818, it was as a novelist that he would henceforth address his age—indeed, as a novelist of a very particular kind. Involving more than a transition from verse to prose, Peacock's literary metamorphosis brought with it a radical change in outlook. If, as one critic has observed, Peacock the poet was "a pure emanation of the Spirit of the Age,"[1] Peacock the novelist was its antithesis. Like the Byron of *Don Juan,* who in rejecting romantic affectation also rejects the earlier Byron of *Childe Harold* and *Manfred,* Peacock seems in his first novel to have succeeded entirely in shedding the romantic persona of his earlier poetry.

Various reasons, biographical and critical, have been offered for this apparently sudden shift in attitude. Although biographical inferences about Peacock are bound to be tentative, it is clear that his friendship with Shelley was one factor in his development as a writer. Through his friend, Peacock came into closer personal contact with the world of letters and ideas, and the social and intellectual interaction between the two friends must have contributed to the growth of both as writers. There were other factors, however, and to claim categorically that "the friendship *made* Peacock," as some critics have,[2] is to deny Peacock the serious consideration as a thinking, conscious artist that Shelley has finally received in this century.

Comedy and Civilization

As early as 1809, while he was writing *The Genius of the Thames,* Peacock had recognized that his response, aesthetic and intellectual, to such things as modern commerce and technology was more complex than conventional verse allowed him to express. In his letter to Hookham, cited in the previous chapter, he at least considers hypothetically the satiric perspective, even while taking the safer role of panegyrist in the poem. Moreover, he expresses some uncertainty about poetry itself, observing in his notes to the poem that "the tutelary spirits, that formerly animated the scenes of nature, still continue to adorn the visions of poetry; though they are now felt only as the creatures of imagination, and no longer possess that influence of real existence, which must have imparted many enviable sensations to the mind of the ancient polytheist" (6:157). Eventually, Peacock would deny modern poetry even this rather qualified affirmation. His last long poem, *Rhododaphne* (1818), is set in ancient Greece, but around its perimeters lurk serious doubts about poetry in the present age: "In ocean's caves no Nereid dwells: / No Oread walks the mountain-dells" (7:29).

This tendency in Peacock's thought would culminate in the ironic, and rather ambiguous, "Four Ages of Poetry," which argues that in a modern, rational society, man loses the imaginative capacity for creating genuine poetry. What was there, then, for the modern artist to do? In *An Essay on the Genius and Writings of Pope* (1782), a work mentioned by Peacock in a letter to Shelley (8:209), Joseph Warton states that the eighteenth-century poet Alexander Pope "early left the more poetical provinces of his art to become a moral, didactic, and satiric poet"—satire being "that species of poetry to which his talent was most powerfully bent."[3] This account of Pope's career has a particular application to Peacock's own, as Peacock himself might have noted, for he had a similar rationale in taking up satire and comedy. Most obviously, like Warton's Pope, he saw simply that his talents lay in this direction. Beyond such essentially personal factors, however, he would also have accepted the historical thesis Warton puts forward in his study, that "if the Moderns have excelled the Ancients in any species of writing, it seems to be in satire."[4]

This view was held by many other eighteenth-century literary theorists besides Warton. In his *History of English Poetry* (1775), for example, Warton's brother Thomas states that "satire is the poetry of a nation highly polished."[5] Such a notion was a commonplace by Peacock's time, but if we are to understand Peacock, we must take into account this historically conditioned view of literature and society, a legacy of the eighteenth-century Enlightenment. Like an

Englightenment historian, Peacock believed that manners and morals were relative, rather than absolute, and that they reflected the
degree of civilization achieved by a society at any given time. It
followed, then, that the literature of a society, no less than its
political and social institutions, similarly reflected that society's
degree of civilization. Thus where the powerful epics of Homer
reflect the turbulent civil conditions of Homeric society, the urbane
satires of Pope are the product of a more stable, polished society.

The "poetry of civilized life" that distinguishes the silver age in
"The Four Ages" is of two kinds: the "imitative," which merely
recasts and polishes the tragic and heroic forms of earlier epochs,
and the "original," which "is chiefly comic, didactic, or satiric"
(8:10). In Peacock's scheme, of course, the classical silver age, which
witnesses the rise of the comic-satiric modes, is succeeded by the
romantic brass age, which takes a retrograde stride back into spurious barbarity. But it should be noted that while Peacock observes
in his essay that, of the silver age's "original" poetry, the "ethical"
and "didactic" forms have become exhausted, he is suggestively
silent regarding comedy and satire. The motto of his second novel,
Melincourt, significantly, is *Vocem Commoedia Tollit,"* "Comedy raises
its voice," and is taken from Horace, whom Peacock praises elsewhere for his "extensive" sympathies (9:353).

Peacock's own comedy, at once genial and eclectic, surely reflects
such sympathies. Just as the Homeric muse in its time, according
to "The Four Ages," gave "the grand outline of things" (8:13), so
must modern literature, if it is to count for anything, keep pace
with the "comprehensive views and enlarged combinations" (8:11)
of its sister arts and sciences. And this, in Peacock's opinion, is
where his contemporaries have failed. Retreating into the ostensibly
more "natural scenes" of the past, they have mistaken "the prominent novelty for the all-important totality" (8:17)—and so must
Peacock have also felt about his own youthful Ossianic imitations
and even the more ambitious poems, such as *The Genius of the Thames*
and *The Philosophy of Melancholy,* which are clearly of the obsolete
"didactic" and "ethical" bent mentioned above.

Peacock would hardly have claimed the Regency as a great age
of comedy and satire—as were the Restoration or the eighteenth
century, for which he had such great affinities—but he certainly
thought it was ripe for such treatment. "There never was any state

of society," he observes in the unfinished "Essay on Fashionable Literature" (1818),

in which there were so many idle persons as there are at present in England, and it happens that these idle persons are for the most part so circumstanced that they can do nothing if they would, and in the next place that they are united in the links of a common interest which, being based in delusion, makes them even more averse than the well-dressed vulgar always are from the free exercise of reason and the bold investigation of truth (8:263-64).

As might be expected, contemporary literature reflects this torpid intellectual climate. Peacock does not name names for the most part, although he does mention Sir Walter Scott, whose historical romances were at that time very popular. Without being entirely dismissive of Scott, Peacock complains that Scott is too careful to keep clear of "opinion" in his works, and concludes that in the fashionable literature of the age, generally, "fancy" rarely ventures into the arena of "opinion." By contrast, past authors such as "Cervantes—Rabelais—Swift—Voltaire—Fielding—have led fancy against opinion" (8:275). It is to these writers, clearly, that Peacock looks for his ideal of a literature of social and intellectual engagement.

The audience for Peacock's poetry, inasmuch as one existed, comprised the frivolous and complacent readership described in "Fashionable Literature." A transition as radical as that from romantic versifier to comic ironist would necessarily entail a radically new audience, or at least a radically changed attitude on the part of Peacock toward his former audience. Whereas Peacock the poet paid court to the conventional tastes of his readers, Peacock the satirist would challenge them, setting "fancy against opinion."

The Novels of Talk

Peacock's fiction may be divided into two groups. The "satiric romances," which include *Maid Marian* and *The Misfortunes of Elphin*, will be dealt with in a subsequent chapter. The other novels, which include *Headlong Hall, Melincourt, Nightmare Abbey, Crotchet Castle,* and *Gryll Grange,* are most frequently called "novels of talk" or "novels of ideas," although neither term is entirely adequate. The "novel of ideas" comprehends numerous works that have little in common with Peacock's novels beyond containing "ideas" in some form. The novels of George Orwell, for example, might be described as "novels of ideas," but they are clearly different from Peacock's in terms of their form. Similarly, there are "novels of talk" in which ideas are not essential, such as those of Ivy Compton-Burnett. One term, then, describes the "content" of Peacock's novels, the other the "form". Unfortunately, to call them "Peacockian novels," perhaps the most accurate term finally, is to beg the question. "Novels of talk" will be used here, if only because it is the term most commonly used to describe this category of Peacock's fiction.

Form.   Described by one commentator as "the most monomorphic little group to be found in literature,"[6] the novels of talk indeed comprise a characteristic body of work. For, surveying this tiny body of work from the first novel, published in 1816, to the last, published in 1861, we find remarkably little variation in the basic pattern. It is a simple enough pattern, and perhaps for that reason Peacock saw no need to tamper with it. Merely gather a diverse group of characters together in a country house, and let them talk. The opinions of these characters should be as opposite as possible, their conflict forming the basis of the novel's development. Plot and action, in the conventional sense, are rudimentary.

The central interest of a Peacockian novel of talk, then, lies in the opinions expressed by its characters. Not surprisingly, Peacock's characters seem, by ordinary fictional standards, rather one-dimensional, for in most cases they are defined entirely by their opinions. Peacock himself provides the best account of this mode of characterization in an essay on the "French Comic Romances":

In respect of presenting or embodying opinion, there are two very distinct classes of comic fictions: one in which the characters are abstractions or embodied classifications, and the implied or embodied opinions the main matter of the work; another, in which the characters are individuals, and the events and the action those of actual life—the opinions, however prominent they may be made, being merely incidental. (9:258)

It is the business of the first class of comic fiction "to stir up and play with opinions." Plot, action, setting, all these elements are secondary. Although, as we will see, they are not nearly as extraneous to the novels' main development as critics often assume, they are subordinate to the play of opinion.

Peacock's novels clearly belong to the first class of comic fiction, their characters seeming to exist solely for the purpose of advancing or refuting an opinion. But if these characters were no more than this—obsessed cranks—it is doubtful that they would hold our interest as much as they do. The monomaniacs are only one element. Indeed, J.B. Priestley identifies three main types of character in Peacock's fiction. First, there are the "crotcheteers," as they are often called, each dominated by a single theory or idée fixé. They are generally minor characters, interesting in few respects beyond whatever intellectual crotchet they possess or are possessed by. Some typical Peacockian crotcheteers are Mr. Chromatic in *Headlong Hall,* who thinks of nothing but music, and Mr. Firedamp in *Crotchet Castle,* who is convinced that all disease can be traced to water. According to Priestley, these characters serve in the novels "as a kind of chorus, hinting at wilder and wilder absurdities and antics of the human mind."[7]

Then there are the caricatures of actual people. These are the most sensitive of Peacock's characterizations, as they trespass on real life (some Shelley and Coleridge scholars still tend to be rather touchy on this matter as it relates to their respective subjects). Certainly, the caricatures of Coleridge—four in all, including Mr. Panscope in *Headlong Hall,* Moley Mystic in *Melincourt,* Mr. Flosky in *Nightmare Abbey,* and Mr. Skionar in *Crotchet Castle*—could hardly be said to represent the man in any genuine sense. They present merely an absurd Tory reactionary dedicated to obscuring every issue behind an impenetrable veil of jargon. (It is worth noting, though, that Peacock never once alludes to Coleridge's tragic personal problems, such as his opium addiction.) The portraits of Shelley—Mr. Forester in *Melincourt* and Scythrop Glowry in *Nightmare Abbey*—are similarly simplistic, drawing on some particular intellectual or aesthetic attitude and building the character around that. Some harsh, and rather sketchy, caricatures appear of Robert Southey and various other figures associated by Peacock with the Tory establishment. But even these are not so much malicious personal portraits as criticisms of the public figure, for Peacock rarely if ever oversteps the line dividing satire and invective. In the preface to an 1837 edition of his novels, he could truthfully deny having "taken any liberties but with public conduct and public opinions" (1:1).

The third category of characters includes those who seem more rounded, or simply more ordinary, than the crotcheteers and the caricatures. These range from fairly bland characters such as Peacock's hosts—Messrs. Crotchet and Gryll, for example, whose primary purpose is to be hospitable to their eccentric guests—to a few of the female characters, such as Lady Clarinda in *Crotchet Castle,* who rival the outspoken and witty women of Shakespeare's comedies. A requisite for civilized comedy, according to George Meredith in his "Essay on Comedy," is "a society of cultivated men and women,"[8] and Peacock's female characters more than fulfill their role.

One trait is shared by all of Peacock's characters, and that is the elegance of their language. Even the most eccentric express their bizarre notions in precise, carefully balanced phrases. The effect is one of drollness and understated irony, which at the same time contributes to the civilized aura that pervades the novels. This is not to suggest that there is no variation in Peacock's language at all. The playful use of language is evident in various connections. Like Rabelais before him, Peacock delights in parodying the jargon of pedantry. In *Headlong Hall* the phrenologist Mr. Cranium defers to the laymen among his listeners by substituting for the technical term "osteosarchaematosplanchnochondroneuromuelous" the more intelligible(?), "osseocarnisanguineoviscericartilaginonervomedullary" (1:109); the various caricatures of Coleridge that recur throughout the novels depend mainly on this sort of verbal burlesque. Related to this is the absurdly abstract language that characterizes slapstick in the novels, such as Mr. Cranium's famous pratfall in *Headlong Hall:* "His ascent being unluckily a little out of the perpendicular, he descended with a proportionate curve from the apex of his projection" (1:88).

Influences.   If finding an adequate term for Peacock's particular fictional form is problematic, the question of literary influence is no less so. Peacock rarely discussed his writing in his letters, and then only in the most general terms. Clearly, his novels do not belong in the mainstream of English literature, but there are points of resemblance between them and the works of other authors. Many of these, some of which Peacock did know, have been suggested as direct influences, although such identifications are bound to be tentative when dealing with a writer as singular as Peacock.

Shelley must have had some influence. "I have in preparation a Novel," Shelley wrote to his publisher in 1810; "it is principally constructed to convey metaphysical & political opinions by way of conversation."[9] Such a work, however, would undoubtedly have been heavily polemical, and thus very different in spirit from those novels Peacock would write. In their basic conception Peacock's novels do indeed convey opinions "by way of conversation"—but not necessarily the opinions of Peacock himself, and this makes all the difference. Peacock's one novel of which Shelley approved whole-heartedly, the didactic *Melincourt,* is the least characteristic, and probably the least liked by modern readers, of the "novels of talk." The opinions put forth in this novel are unequivocally those of its author and, finally, of its author's friend. By contrast, in the other "novels of talk," and in the "satiric romances" as well, Peacock cannot be pinned down nearly so easily.

Because talk is such an important element in these novels, much more important than such conventional elements of fiction as plot and character, one likely literary model is the dialogue. Classical authors like Plato and Lucian worked in this form, and the dialogue was used by a number of eighteenth-century writers, such as John Dryden and the Earl of Shaftsbury. "Dialogue writing is nothing else but conversation in writing," according to Lord Monboddo, a favorite author of Peacock's, "not conversation however upon the ordinary affairs of life, but upon matters of art or science."[10] The dialogue, as Monboddo defines it, is somewhat more elaborate than we might expect, for "it has a fable, characters, manners, incidents, and scenery too, and in short, every thing belonging to a dramatic piece."[11] Peacock's first sustained efforts in comedy, we recall, were his versified farces, which anticipate the novels in many respects.

Peacock probably had some actual fictional forebears as well. The eighteenth-century French *conte* has frequently been suggested as a possible prototype. In these works, as in Peacock's novels, characters often embody opinions, and discussion is usually more prominent than action. Voltaire, Diderot, and Marmontel are authors who might have influenced Peacock. As Carl Dawson points out, however, we need not go further than English literature to find a similar tradition of "conversational novels" developing in the late eighteenth century.[12] Thomas Holcroft, George Walker, Thomas Day, and Mrs. Inchbald are among the writers cited by Dawson, but two others, Isaac Disraeli and Robert Bage, are serious contenders as Peacockian prototypes.

Robert Bage's *Mount Henneth* (1781) is set in a country house in Wales where a genial host has gathered together a diverse company for the sake of friendly conversation. A later novel, *Hermspronge*

(1796), anticipates Peacock even more closely, employing genuine dramatic dialogues in the manner of Peacock's novels, although it should be noted that both Peacock and Bage may have had a common source in the French contes, particularly those of Voltaire. Isaac Disraeli, father of the novelist and prime minister, employs dramatic dialogues between recognizable public persons in his *Vaurien* (1797). Another work by Disraeli, *Flim-Flams* (1806), consists of miscellaneous satirical sketches in which Disraeli ridicules a number of current fads such as phrenology and landscape gardening—two topics that would concern Peacock in his first novel.

Peacock has also been included under the heading of Menippean satire. This broad category comprehends works by authors as diverse as Rabelais and Herman Melville, and is mainly distinguished by an emphasis on intellectual attitudes rather than on character in the conventional sense. Northrop Frye gives the definitive account of Menippean satire in his *Anatomy of Criticism:*

The Menippean satire deals less with people as such than with mental attitudes. Pedants, bigots, cranks, parvenus, virtuosi, enthusiasts, rapacious and incompetent professional men of all kinds, are handled in terms of their occupational approach to life as distinct from their social behaviour. The Menippean satire thus . . . differs from the novel in its characterization, which is stylized rather than naturalistic, and presents people as mouthpieces of the ideas they represent. . . . The novelist sees evil and folly as social diseases, but the Menippean satirist sees them as diseases of the intellect, as a kind of maddened pedantry. [13]

Frye offers not only a satisfying premise for the satiric emphases of Peacock's novels but, to a limited extent, a premise for their structure as well. Menippean satire is essentially a medley form, incorporating, in what may seem to be a slapdash manner, everything from lengthy digressions on sundry apparently unrelated topics to verse interludes. A "magpie instinct to collect facts" and "the ironic use of erudition"[14] are two related characteristics of Menippean satire that describe at once treatment and form in Peacock's satire.

In the end, however, perhaps "Peacockian" does best describe Peacock's novels of talk, for there is nothing quite like them in literature. Their country-house settings, according to Dawson, are "emblems of a state of mind,"[15] and it is this intangible quality, neither purely a matter of form nor of content, but of attitude, that finally distinguishes them. Insular and self-contained, essentially products of their creator's idealism, they offer a civilized alternative to the aesthetic and intellectual barbarism of the world outside.

Headlong Hall (1816)

Probably by the autumn of 1815 Peacock had abandoned work on his mythological poem "Ahrimanes," and was already putting the final touches on *Headlong Hall*. (Indeed, a portion of the novel can be found on one of the blank pages of the "Ahrimanes" MS.) Although it is difficult to assign exact dates, it is likely Peacock began *Headlong Hall* when he moved to Marlow earlier in 1815. Appearing in late 1815, the novel's first edition bore the date 1816 on its title page. Unlike some of the previous volumes of poetry, it was published anonymously, a common practice at the time. Few details are known about the actual composition of *Headlong Hall*. Some of its characters and situations are taken from the farces, *The Dilettanti* and *The Three Doctors*. Its rural setting, its curious admixture of slapstick and fast-paced dialogue, probably owe a partial debt to them as well.

But if it borrowed in particulars from these earlier works, in its general conception *Headlong Hall* marked a new direction for Peacock. It was a fully formed example of the works that would soon follow, in every respect a typical Peacockian novel of talk. Recognizing this sureness of execution, the *Critical Review* said of the anonymous author "we suspect him to be no novice" (1:lxiv). Other journals, *La Belle Assemblée* and the *Eclectic Review,* and to a lesser extent the *Monthly Review,* were similarly approving, although the diarist Henry Crabb Robinson privately felt that "the commonplaces of the literators [*sic*] of the day are not preserved from being tiresome by original humour or wit, so that the book is very dull."[16] Described by a modern critic as "a rickety prototype to be drastically modified,"[17] *Headlong Hall* nevertheless sets a pattern that remains remarkably constant throughout the subsequent novels of talk, notwithstanding the inevitable development of Peacock's technique. While not the best of the novels, then, *Headlong Hall* is in many ways the most characteristic, "a battle-ground of opinion from first to last," as Carl Van Doren observes.[18]

Philosophers and dilettanti. Indeed, the battle begins almost as soon as Peacock introduces his major disputants in Chapter 1. They are Messrs. Foster, Escot, and Jenkison, all three philosophers and each embodying a particular intellectual attitude. Mr. Foster is a "perfectibilian," an optimist who believes that everything is tending toward the best; the pessimistic Mr. Escot, who is a "deteriorationist," holds the opposing view that everything is tending toward the worst. Occupying a middle position is Mr. Jenkison, the "statu-quo-ite," who believes that everything "remains exactly and perpetually *in statu quo*" (1:11). Accompanying these three is one Reverend Doctor Gaster, who, though neither a philosopher nor a man of taste, is nevertheless a prodigious gastronome, sufficient reason in itself for his inclusion in the book. He is also the first of a line of venal and foolish clergymen in Peacock's satire.

The novel opens to find these characters traveling in a coach to Headlong Hall, the country seat of the Headlongs, an old Welsh noble family that can trace its lineage back to before the Flood. The present Squire Headlong, while pursuing all the usual activities of a country peer, such as shooting, hunting, racing, and drinking, has also got into the rather more unusual habit of reading books, and has been "seized with a violent passion to be thought a philosopher and a man of taste" (1:7). Accordingly, he has decided to surround himself with philosophers and men of taste at Headlong Hall. The four coach passengers are on their way to sample Squire Headlong's hospitality in exchange for their intellectual wares.

In chapter 3 we are introduced to one Marmaduke Milestone, another of the squire's guests and "a picturesque landscape gardener of the first celebrity" (1:23). Based on a famous landscape designer of the day, Humphrey Repton, Mr. Milestone has come to Headlong Hall with the intention of persuading the squire "to put his romantic pleasure-grounds under a process of improvement" (1:23). Other guests include Mr. Cranium and his lovely daughter Cephalis. As his name is meant to suggest, Mr. Cranium is an authority on phrenology, a now-discredited nineteenth-century pseudoscience which claimed a correspondence between one's character and the shape of one's skull. Mr. Cranium arrives with a bag of skulls to be used for the purpose of illustrating a lecture on phrenology.

Some more minor crotcheteers arrive soon after. Mr. Gall and Mr. Treacle are critics, representatives of the age's very powerful and politically partisan literary press. The major journals were the Whiggish *Edinburgh Review,* the Tory *Quarterly Review,* and the ultra-Tory *Blackwood's Magazine,* at whose hands all of the romantic poets suffered some abuse. (In his fragmentary "Essay on Fashionable Literature" Peacock would defend Coleridge's "Christabel" against a savage, and anonymous, attack in the *Edinburgh Review.*) Whatever the real-life originals of Gall and Treacle—both Francis Jeffrey of the *Edinburgh* and William Gifford of the *Quarterly* come to mind—their respective names are clearly meant to suggest the less-than-disinterested nature of periodical criticism at that time, which Mr. Escot later denounces as "a species of shop, where panegyric and defamation are sold, wholesale, retail, and for exportation" (1:43). Two poets who accompany Gall and Treacle, Mr. Nightshade and Mr. Mac Laurel, are in suspiciously close association with their critics.

Among some later arrivals at Headlong Hall is Mr. Cornelius Chromatic, a "scientific" musician, who brings with him his two daughters Miss Tenorina and Miss Graziosa. Sir Patrick O'Prism is "a dilettante painter of high renown" (1:27), who is accompanied by his maiden aunt, a Miss Philomela Poppyseed, a prolific compounder of fashionable novels often identified with a popular novelist of the day named Amelia Opie. In any case, her novels seem to be written "for the express purpose of supporting every species of superstition and prejudice" (1:27–28). Finally, there is Peacock's first, and crudest, caricature of Coleridge, Mr. Panscope, "the chemical, botanical, geological, astronomical, mathematical, metaphysical, meteorological, anatomical, physiological, galvanistical, musical, pictorial, bibliographical, critical philospher." Mr. Panscope "had run through the whole circle of the sciences, and understood them all equally well" (1:28).

Having gathered his guests together, then, and provided them with comfortable lodgings and pleasant scenery, Peacock can get down to his real business as a novelist, which is to give these characters an opportunity to talk. A walk through the grounds of Headlong Hall in chapter 4 prompts a debate between Marmaduke Milestone and Sir Patrick O'Prism on the "picturesque" and the "beautiful," which Mr. Gall attempts to resolve with his fine critical discrimination:

"Allow me," said Mr. Gall. "I distinguish the picturesque and the beautiful, and I add to them, in the laying out of grounds, a third and distinct character, which I call *unexpectedness.*"

"Pray, sir," said Mr. Milestone, "by what name do you distinguish this character, when a person walks round the grounds for the second time?" (1:31–32).

Meanwhile, the "three philosophers," Escot, Foster, and Jenkison, debate the pros and cons of progress. As often happens in Peacock's novels, such controversies are resolved only by the announcement of dinner. But, of course, the repast that follows merely provides further occasion for debate.

The plot of *Headlong Hall* turns on a love interest. Where Miss Cephalis Cranium is concerned, significantly, Mr. Escot "could imagine the possibility of one change for the better, even in this terrestrial theatre of universal deterioration" (1:26). Unfortunately, an obstacle exists in the person of Miss Cephalis's father, Mr. Cranium, who bears Escot a grudge for laughing at one of his craniological dissertations. A change for the better is imminent, however. Mr. Milestone's "improvements" to Squire Headlong's grounds involve a quantity of gunpowder, and an ill-timed explosion sends Mr. Cranium toppling into a lake from which Mr. Escot rescues him, thus earning his reluctant gratitude. (Mr. Cranium's resistance is finally overcome when Escot gives him as a gift an over-sized skull which is allegedly that of a legendary Welsh hero named Cadwallader.) After several chapters of further debate and a fancy dress ball in chapter 13, Peacock inevitably gets round to marrying Mr. Escot and Miss Cephalis, along with several other couples, bringing the novel to "a happy, an easy, an incredibly tidy end."[19]

The perfectibility of man. *Headlong Hall*'s central debate concerns the idea of progress. Put simply, is progress good or bad? Still current today, this debate gained impetus from a rapid expansion of commerce and manufacturing during the eighteenth century. Where formerly orthodox economic doctrine stressed simplicity and frugality, the eighteenth century's new prosperity resulted in an increased consumption of luxuries, and with this came the need to justify such consumption. Mandeville's famous defense of luxury in his *Fable of the Bees* (1714) sparked a controversy that raged on through the century in periodical literature, in moral philosophy, even in fiction.[20] Against the new economic doctrines were opposed classical ethics, Christian theology, the testimony of travelers among primitive tribes, and perhaps most crucially the rationalism of the early eighteenth century which prescribed nature as moral norm.

Thus if apologists for capitalism like Mandeville and Adam Smith lauded the new prosperity, a conservative and mainly popular faction opposed it and denounced it as evil and corrupting. "It is admired, and it is blamed," Adam Ferguson observed of luxury; "it is treated as ornamental and useful; and it is proscribed as vice."[21]

Peacock presents the broad outlines of this controversy through his "three philosophers," Escot, Foster, and Jenkison. Their debate occupies the foreground of *Headlong Hall,* subsuming all other elements of the novel into an overarching preoccupation with the pros and cons of progress. Landscape design, phrenology, periodical criticism, fashionable literature, even marriage, are all implicated in this controversy.[22] The opposing positions taken in this debate are the usual ones. In chapter 7, for example, Foster and Escot view a thriving manufacturing community at Tremedoc: where Foster sees positive proof of progress in the scene—"employment and existence thus given to innumerable families, and the multiplied comforts and conveniences of life diffused over the whole community"— Escot sees in it only evidence of "selfish and ruinous profusion" (1:77).

Foster and Escot have been identified with Shelley and Peacock respectively, and the complacent Jenkison with Thomas Jefferson Hogg. Peacock's association with Shelley and his circle undoubtedly left its imprint on *Headlong Hall,* but the influence is better seen in terms of generalized intellectual attitudes than of specific personalities. While Shelley certainly shared aspects of Mr. Foster's rosy optimism, he would have drawn the line at praising modern commerce, as his objections to such a strain in Peacock's earlier *Genius of the Thames* clearly demonstrate. Moreover, many of Mr. Escot's views have been drawn directly from the notes to *Queen Mab* (1813), and thus also reflect many of Shelley's own views at this time.

Indeed, Escot is a virtual anthology of primitivistic thought. His vegetarianism he seems to have picked up from J. S. Newton of Bracknell, probably by way of Shelley, who cites the former in the notes to *Queen Mab.* (In his Shelley memoirs, Peacock recalled how he managed to wean Shelley from his vegetable regimen for one week, during which Shelley enjoyed one of his few periods of health.) Escot's curious belief that modern man has greatly declined in physical stature since a distant heroic age is drawn from Lord Monboddo (1714–1799), an eccentric Scottish author and a true crotcheteer in his own right, whose multitomed works were favorite reading for Peacock. Monboddo and a more famous eighteenth-century prim-itivist, Jean Jacques Rousseau, have similarly provided Escot with his Natural Man, that mythical epitome of primitive goodness, against whom Escot measures modern man's physical and moral degeneracy.

Foster's ancestry is likewise a notable one. Again, Shelley is the most likely immediate influence, for *Queen Mab* is essentially a paean to social progress, its primitivistic tendencies notwithstanding, and Shelley's mentor here was William Godwin. All but forgotten today, Godwin's weighty *Political Justice* (1793) was during the decade of its publication a bible to social and political reformers. "Man," according to Godwin, " . . . is a being of progressive nature, and capable of unlimited improvement."[23]

Though ameliorist and deteriorationist respectively, Foster and Escot share a common assumption about human nature. This is that man is characterized by what Rousseau termed a *"faculté de se per-fectionner,"* or a faculty of "perfectibility," namely, an innate ten-dency toward improvement. Given currency by Rousseau, this term eventually became the catchword of such apostles of progress as Godwin, and so had widely diverging applications, depending on who used it. For Godwin "intellect has a perpetual tendency to proceed," and this is for the best. Rousseau, although he distin-guishes man from the brute by "the faculty of self-improvement," believes that it is man's perfectibility which will finally lead to man's downfall.[24] Contrary to what we might expect, then, to say that man is "perfectible," in this technical sense, is not to suggest that he will ever achieve perfection; only that he will continually strive for it. Mr. Foster is obviously convinced of "the perfectibility of the species" (1:16), and while Escot seems at times to deny altogether the notion of perfectibility, he does so probably by er-roneously taking it to mean absolute perfection rather than, as both Rousseau and Godwin define it, simply the tendency to change perpetually, whether for better or worse. For Foster things "may, and therefore will, be changed for the better," where for Escot "every change is for the worse" (1:103), but neither of them doubts the inevitability of some kind of change.

Headlong Hall is more than just a symposium on progress in the abstract, however. In chapter 2, while Escot, Foster, and Jenkison argue in their coach about the virtues and evils of commercial society, an actual torrent of packages is pouring into Headlong Hall in preparation for their arrival—"books, wine, cheese, globes, mathematical instruments, turkeys, telescopes," all arriving "with infinite rapidity, and in inexhaustible succession" (1:14). It is no coincidence, surely, that Escot and Foster debate the consequences of just such a profusion of luxuries in modern society as they view the factories and mills at Tremedoc. Elsewhere in the novel, too, luxury manifests itself, for better or worse, in concrete form. The squire's guests—novelists, phrenologists, metaphysicians, musicians, landscapers, all frequently shown pursuing the distractions provided at Headlong Hall—are themselves both the purveyors and the consumers of luxury in this society.

The landscape controversy.   One of these luxuries in particular, landscape design, plays a central role in the novel, effectively linking theme and action. Indeed, a farcical history of civil society outlined by Marmaduke Milestone in chapter 4 indicates the specific form that *Headlong Hall's* satire of human perfectibility will take:

"One age . . . has brought to light the treasures of ancient learning; a second has penetrated into the depths of metaphysics; a third has brought to perfection the science of astronomy; but it was reserved for the exclusive genius of the present times, to invent the noble art of picturesque gardening, which has given, as it were, a new tint to the complexion of nature, and a new outline to the physiognomy of the universe!" (1:30)

As mentioned earlier, Marmaduke Milestone is a caricature of the landscaper Humphrey Repton, or rather of Repton's highly formalistic theories on landscape design. During the 1790s Repton was attacked by critics who preferred a more natural approach to landscape to the typical Repton prospect, "one dull vapid smooth and tranquil scene."[25] According to these critics, nature in its rude, primitive state was full of picturesque possibilities and preferable to the clipped and shaved results of Repton's "improvements."

But the landscape controversy in *Headlong Hall* has more than merely topical interest. While appearing as a character in Peacock's earlier farce, *The Three Doctors,* Marmaduke Milestone says of the servant of one Squire Hippy: "That fellow's an uncivilized goat— a mountain-savage—a wild man of the woods. Wants shaving and polishing. As much in need of improvement as the place he inhabits. Great capabilities here" (7:404). It is not clear whether

Mr. Milestone detects these "great capabilities" in Squire Hippy's servant or in his grounds. It could easily be in both, for in an eighteenth- or early nineteenth-century context "capabilities" is a very pregnant term. If the landscaper could see infinite "capabilities" in a rude, unpolished setting, so also the philosopher or the moralist could be confident of similar "capabilities" in man in even his most primitive state. The term, then, denotes a potential for progress, an innate faculty evident, according to the phrenologist Mr. Cranium, in even the bumps and protuberances of a man's skull—in a word, perfectibility. Upon his arrival at Headlong Hall, Mr. Milestone sees "great capabilities," but as is the case with both the grounds and servants of Squire Hippy, it all wants "polishing" (1:25).

The "improvements" attempted by Mr. Milestone in chapter 8 ("The Tower") are clearly a practical illustration of the issue debated by Foster and Escot.[26] Earlier, in chapter 4, while Milestone has surveyed Squire Headlong's grounds to ascertain their "capabilities," Escot, Foster, and Jenkison have been discussing the capabilities of man as they view a lone boatman from the excellent (from a picturesque point of view) prospect of "a projecting point of rock" (1:32). Later in chapter 7, directly preceding "The Tower," the three philosophers view the shattered magnificence of the Vale of Llandberris, and their discussion follows a familiar pattern. To Escot's "philosophic eye" the results of some past universal cataclysm are evident in the scene before him, with its "vast fragments of stone" and "perpendicular rocks, broken into the wildest forms of fantastic magnificence" (1:72). Foster characteristically argues against Escot's gloomy belief that this fallen condition is permanent, and predicts a future "precession of the equinoxes," which will bring about a vast improvement of the earth's state and coincide with an equal improvement in human nature (1:72–73). However, the debate ends abruptly, interrupted by a cataclysm of less than universal dimensions, the explosion that nearly sends Mr. Cranium to a watery grave.

More than being merely a gratuitous piece of slapstick, the explosion accompanying Squire Headlong's improvements bears a syllogistic relation to the debate on progress that occupies the novel's level of discourse. Indeed, if the three philosophers talk about man's innately progressive nature, and posit some inexorable force operating behind all change—whether for better or for worse, a force innate in man and nature—it is their host, Squire Headlong, who actively demonstrates this hypothesis, effectively embodying the concept of perfectibility.

The squire and his schemes form the background of necessity against which *Headlong Hall*'s action takes place. Squire Headlong is at once the descendant of an ancient and venerable family, and a creditable specimen of man in his polished state. Thus, if he can trace his lineage to before the Great Flood, he can also say with all the complacency of the civilized man, "I happen to be more enlightened than any of my ancestors were" (1:139). Neither a philosopher nor a moralist, and possessing none of the eccentric views that distinguish the novel's other characters, he is in no way remarkable save in his seeming inability to stay still for even a moment:

In all the thoughts, words, and actions of Squire Headlong, there was a remarkable alacrity of progression, which almost annihilated the interval between conception and execution. He was utterly regardless of obstacles, and seemed to have expunged their very name from his vocabulary. His designs were never nipped in their infancy by the contemplation of those trivial difficulties which often turn awry the current of enterprise; and, though the rapidity of his movements was sometimes arrested by a more formidable barrier, either naturally existing in the pursuit he had undertaken, or created by his own impetuosity, he seldom failed to succeed either in knocking it down or cutting his way through it. (1:83).

The consequences of this "headlong" drive to move forward at any cost are amply evident in the enthusiasm with which the squire attacks Mr. Milestone's landscaping project, and in the ensuing catastrophe.

The "philosophical balance." To Escot's "philosophic eye" the landscape fiasco is no doubt yet another proof of the fatal Promethean impulse in man. Nevertheless, the novel goes inexorably on to a comic resolution. Moreover, just as the catastrophe that overtakes the squire's "improvements" is meant as a practical exposition of Escot's and Foster's theoretical ruminations on progress, so it also serves to forward *Headlong Hall*'s love interest—and in a manner entirely relevant, and essential, to the novel's subject of progress.

Escot it is, of course, who rescues Mr. Cranium from drowning as a consequence of the squire's ill-fated project. This heroic action is at least as instrumental in redeeming modern society as the landscape disaster itself is in discrediting it. Much earlier, during one of his diatribes against civilized man—the "sophisticated, cold-blooded, mechanical, calculating slave of Mammon" (1:36)—Escot illustrates his argument by imagining himself in the place of a drowning man. The unsophisticated man, he claims, would rescue him, whereas the modern philosopher, with his wholly detached view of the incident, would not (1:36). Like Rousseau, who declares that "a state of reflection is a state contrary to nature,"[27] Escot praises "the original, unthinking, unscientific, unlogical savage" (1:36). Yet Escot himself is preeminently a creature of reflection. His primitivist views are no less the product of his thinking nature than is the criminal inaction of the modern rationalist in his hypothetical example. Indeed, as Jenkison points out in chapter 13, Escot's savage man, in order to appreciate his superior moral nature, would have to be transferred "from his wild and original state to a very advanced stage of intellectual progression" (1:122). Ironically, then, it is Escot, his own advanced stage of intellectual progression notwithstanding, who performs the benevolent act of rescuing a drowning man.

Moreover, he marries that man's daughter. Prior to the quadruple marriage ceremony that concludes the novel, Squire Headlong infers from Escot's happiness at the prospect of married life, that "there is an amelioration in the state of the sensitive man" (1:147). Escot is reluctant to disavow his deteriorationist thesis—although symbolically he appears to have done so by giving up the skull of Cadwallader (to him a reproach to modern man's punyness) to Cranium for his daughter's hand (1:147)—but his position has been considerably qualified by this point.

In fact, pessimism and optimism alike are rather beside the point finally. Necessity, that inexorable chain of cause and effect, which has turned awry the squire's attempted "improvements" to his grounds and is likewise behind the various scenes of progress alternately censured and praised by Escot and Foster, brings about the multiple marriages of the novel's conventional comic ending. If Mr. Cranium intially refuses his daughter's hand to Mr. Escot—he argues that "they are all equally creatures of necessity," and that no moral significance can thus be attached to his rescue by Escot—Squire Headlong replies in kind, countering that the two lovers "are necessitated to love one another," and that, with or without

Mr. Cranium's assent, their marriage is "inherent in the eternal fitness of things" (1:144–45).

Significantly, it is Mr. Jenkison, the statu-quo-ite, who has the last word in this very talkative novel, concluding that the scales of his "philosophical balance" remain "equiponderant" (1:154). Is this Peacock's last word? When set against the perspective of the past— and the past is used in exactly this way in *Headlong Hall*, as a "perspective" in the manner of landscape design—the modern age is found wanting. Yet Peacock's first novel is hardly a wholesale denunciation of progress. There are signs of change for the better in *Headlong Hall*—in the marriages that close the novel, indeed in the unmistakable aura of civilization which even in the most hectic of situations is never entirely absent. Equiponderant? Perhaps, although there seems always in Peacock to be some slight overbalancing in favor of the optimistic view, in the personal sphere at least. A passage from Volney's *Ruins,* a work cited in the notes to "Ahrimanes," expresses perfectly the optimism, tempered by experience, that informs *Headlong Hall:*

By the law of sensibility, man as inevitably tends to render himself happy as the flame to mount, the stone to descend, or the water to find its level. His obstacle is his ignorance, which misleads him in the means, and deceives him in causes and effects. He will enlighten himself by experience, go right by dint of errors, grow wise and good because it is in his interest to be so.[28]

Chapter Four

Melincourt and *Nightmare Abbey:* Two Responses to Shelley

If *Headlong Hall* bears the unmistakable impress of Peacock's friend-ship with Shelley, *Melincourt* (1817) and *Nightmare Abbey* (1818) provide an intriguing commentary on the personal and intellectual dynamics of this literary friendship. Shelley appears in both works, as *Melincourt*'s Mr. Forester and as *Nightmare Abbey*'s Scythrop Glowry. Neither characterization could be described as fully realized, but each represents a telling response by Peacock to the influence of his friend. In *Melincourt* Peacock embraces wholeheartedly the ideal of social and political engagement associated with the Shelleyan poet-legislator and embodied in Forester. By *Nightmare Abbey,* however, Peacock's more habitually ironic perspective asserts itself, and the result is the absurd figure of Scythrop Glowry. But *Melincourt* and *Nightmare Abbey* amount to much more than this rather schematic summary suggests. Together and separately, they constitute a valu-able analysis of Shelley and the psychology of his age.

Melincourt (1817)

"Peacock is the author of Headlong Hall," Shelley wrote in De-cember 1816 to his radical associate Leigh Hunt, who had evidently read Peacock's first novel:

He expresses himself much pleased by your approbation—indeed it is an approbation which many would be happy to acquire!—He is not writing 'Melincourt' in the same style, but, as I judge, far superior to Headlong Hall.—He is an aimiable [*sic*] man of great learning, considerable taste, an enemy to every shape of tyranny & superstitious imposture.[1]

It is not known whether Hunt thought the finished novel as good as Shelley had predicted it would be, or whether indeed he ever read it. Shelley, however, was not disappointed. Comparing *Melincourt* to the novels that preceded and followed it—*Headlong Hall* and *Nightmare Abbey*—he felt that it had "more of the true spirit, and an object less indefinite."[2]

By "more of the true spirit" Shelley clearly meant that Peacock had taken up the radical cause. "An object less indefinite" is vaguer, but it may refer to the explicit nature of the novel's satire. Peacock is at his most uncharacteristically unequivocal in *Melincourt*. Where the earlier *Headlong Hall* leaves the reader guessing about the author's specific views—Escot seems at first glance to provide some bearings, but just how seriously does Peacock take him?—*Melincourt* presents no such problems. Its satire is, in Priestley's depreciating phrase, "single-edged."[3] Where *Headlong Hall* is characterized by crisp, witty dialogue and an ironic elusiveness on the part of its author, *Melincourt* states ideas and opinions both plainly and, as is all too often the case in this the longest of Peacock's novels, tediously. Moreover, it is highly topical. Electoral malpractice, the issue of paper money, West Indian slavery, Malthusianism, and a host of other specific concerns of the day form the substance of *Melincourt's* satire. Consequently, the novel may seem dated to a modern reader.

But it was this very timeliness that ensured it would be controversial when it first appeared. Advertised in the second edition of *Headlong Hall* in the summer of 1816, *Melincourt* appeared in early 1817 to a predictably partisan reception. The conservative *British Critic* detected in it "the cloven foot of infidelity" and devoted a full twelve pages to dismissing the novel as "miserable trash."[4] In contrast, a liberal organ like the *Monthly Magazine* was happy to pronounce it the work of "a philosopher, a patriot, and a man of taste" (1:lxxi). Today it is generally assumed that Shelley's partiality for *Melincourt* was due more to his endorsement of the novel's political commitment than to critical acumen; and it is the influence of Shelley himself to which critics have attributed this spirit of engagement. The consensus is largely that *Melincourt* falls short as a novel in proportion as it fails to render the Shelleyan strain in convincingly imaginative terms.[5] Nevertheless, this novel presents the most direct exposition we have of the views of an author usually reluctant to reveal his views directly.

Satire and romance.   *Melincourt* has been likened by Marilyn Butler to a medieval romance, its loose, picaresque structure providing the framework for a satirically modified chivalric quest.[6]

Chapter 1 opens to find the novel's heroine besieged in a castle by a rout of fortune-seeking suitors. Anthelia Melincourt, "at the age of twenty-one, was mistress of herself and of ten thousand a year, and of a very ancient and venerable castle in one of the wildest valleys in Westmoreland [*sic*]" (2:5). That she is "mistress of herself" is due to the liberal views of her late father, who "maintained the heretical notion that women are, or at least may be, rational beings" (2:9), and who nourished his daughter's mind on the natural scenes of their Westmorland home and on the Italian chivalric poets of the sixteenth century. Anthelia is an unworldly and idealistic young woman whose notions of love, "altogether theoretical" (2:12), are unlikely to be realized in a modern age.

Indeed, chivalric idealism and modern expedience form the satiric poles of this novel. They are elements not easily reconciled, although some suitors gathered at Melincourt Castle in chapter 8 are willing to try. Informed by Anthelia that "the spirit of the age of chivalry, manifested in the forms of modern life, would constitute the only character on which she could fix her affections" (2:85), these characters succeed only in revealing their own unfitness. One of them is a foolish and conceited young peer named Lord Anophel Achthar. When his tutor explains to him that the spirit of chivalry involves notions of Truth and Liberty, disinterested benevolence, and the subversion of tyranny, he recognizes immediately "all the ingredients of a rank Jacobin" (2:85). There is also a suitor based on Sir Walter Scott, Mr Derrydown, whose notions of chivalry are replete with archaic usages and folk legends gleaned from his antiquarian researches—the mere "forms" of chivalry rather than its "spirit."

Significantly, this group of suitors does not include the novel's hero. Although he lives in the vicinity of Melincourt Castle, Mr. Sylvan Forester is unacquainted with its lovely owner, and at any rate would never deign to pursue the hand of any woman for mere considerations of fortune. Thus he is an idealist; like Anthelia, he seeks a mate who will fulfill his notions of intellectual and moral excellence. Forester is traditionally identified as Shelley, whom he certainly resembles in his views. He is a progressive in his politics and a primitivist in his moral philosophy, essentially combining the idealism and the skepticism that characterized Shelley (and which, incidentally, find separate embodiments in *Headlong Hall*'s Messrs. Foster and Escot).

Mr. Forester's household is rather unusual in that it includes an elegantly dressed orangoutan from the jungles of Angola whom Mr. Forester has adopted as a ward. Peacock has constructed this curious character, one of his most memorable, from a number of sources such as Lord Monboddo, and the naturalists Buffon and Linnaeus. Like his authorities, Peacock presents this creature as "a specimen of the natural and original man" (2:52)—in short, the noble savage. Possessed of impeccable manners and many elegant accomplishments, Sir Oran Haut-ton—"ton" was a Regency cant term denoting a fashionable bearing—serves as a virtuous foil to the corrupt society depicted in *Melincourt*. Moreover, as Mr. Forester informs one astonished character, Sir Oran will soon stand for Parliament as the Honorable Member for the borough of Onevote.

A frequent visitor to this curious household is one Mr. Fax. Described by Forester as "the bearer of the torch of dispassionate truth"(2:73), this character is based on Thomas Malthus, a prominent political economist of the period. Malthus's famous "principle of population," that population increases at a much faster rate than subsistence, is Mr. Fax's ruling obsession.

Unlike the characters of *Headlong Hall,* who stay in one place and talk, *Melincourt's* characters seem constantly to be on the move. If they sometimes pause for a moment at Melincourt Castle, nominally the focal point of the novel, they are soon whisked off somewhere else according to the dictates of Peacock's wide-ranging satire. They do talk, however, and the novel does contain a few symposia in the manner of *Headlong Hall.* In chapter 8, as we have seen already, Anthelia's suitors gather at Melincourt to debate the concept of chivalry. An after-dinner symposium in chapter 16, again at Melincourt, focuses on the venality of the literary world. But the greater bulk of the discussion is between Forester and Fax, who manage to cover a great deal of ground, both literally and figuratively, for they not only discuss the political and social abuses of the age, but witness them firsthand.

Electoral corruption is targeted in chapters 21 and 22, where we get a vivid, and quite authentic, glimpse of how election campaigns were conducted at the time. This episode depicts a campaign to elect no less than two members of Parliament to represent the borough of Onevote with its population of one, while nearby the populous city of Novote has no parliamentary representation at all. Known as "rotten boroughs," political ridings like Onevote were a convenient means by which wealthy and influential landowners could have their interests represented in Parliament. This particular campaign ends in a riot precipitated by the morally outraged Sir Oran. In chapter 27 the desperate plight of agricultural laborers and the destructive greed of contemporary landholders are condemned in the light of Mr. Forester's liberal practices as a landlord. West Indian slavery receives due attention at the Anti-Saccharine Fête held in chapter 27. Peacock himself is said to have boycotted sugar as a protest against the use of slave labor in the West Indian plantations.

That Forester and Anthelia are destined for each other is clear from the start. The two meet following an incident in chapter 10 in which Sir Oran rescues Anthelia from perishing in a violent mountain torrent. Each immediately sees in the other a reflection of his or her ideal lover. Complications arise, however, in the form of one of Anthelia's mercenary suitors, Lord Anophel, who conspires with the aid of the Reverend Mr. Grovelgrub to abduct Anthelia for his wife. A first abduction attempt, in chapter 18, is foiled by Sir Oran. If H.F.B. Brett-Smith is correct, Peacock originally intended *Melincourt* to end following the Anti-Saccharine Fête with the marriage of Forester and Anthelia.[7] However, a second, and this time successful, kidnapping bid postpones for a time both this wedding and the novel's conclusion, as Mr. Forester searches the countryside for his abducted fiancée.

Although the expedient of a second kidnapping attempt is unconvincing in terms of *Melincourt*'s overall structure, it does provide Peacock with a chance to include a memorable satire of Coleridge. The Cimmerian Lodge episode in chapter 31 appears to have been provoked by the publication in late 1816 of the *Statesman's Manual,* a conservative tract on politics and religion by Coleridge. During the course of their search for Anthelia, Mr. Forester and his party accept the hospitality of "the poeticopolitical, rhapsodicoprosaical, deisidaemoniacoparadoxographical, pseudolatreiological, transcendental meteorosophist," Moley Mystic, Esquire, of Cimmerian Lodge (2:328). Situated on what its proprietor calls "the *Island of Pure Intelligence,*" Cimmerian Lodge is a place of fog and darkness—and appropriately so, for Moley Mystic himself is essentially a satiric amalgam of Coleridge's obscurer utterances, mainly gleaned from the *Statesman's Manual,* although the episode also contains a short parody of *The Ancient Mariner:* The fog was here, the fog was there, / The fog was all around (2:333).

Moley Mystic is a reactionary of the most extreme type, dismissing reason and clarity with contempt, and advocating a return to feudal ignorance. The episode ends on a note of slapstick when Mr. Mystic, following a particularly violent harangue, retires for the night only to be blown out of his bedchambers by a violent explosion ignited by his candle and an unstopped gas tube. The sententious Mr. Forester reads into the incident "a warning to the apostles of superstitious chimaera and political fraud" (2:342), concluding that such conflagrations are an inevitable result of political obscurantism.

A related episode occurs in chapter 39, where Mr. Forester and his friends run across a cabal of Tory apologists gathered at the aptly named Mainchance Villa. Caricatures appear here of Robert Southey (Mr. Feathernest) and William Wordsworth (Mr. Paperstamp—so called because Wordsworth held a sinecure position as examiner of stamps for Westmorland), as well as of such conservatively partisan reviewers as William Gifford (Mr. Vamp) and John Wilson Croker (Mr. Killthedead). The politician and Tory polemicist George Canning appears as Mr. Anyside Antijack, whose surname alludes to his association with a reactionary satirical journal entitled the *Anti-Jacobin Review*. Interspersed with such episodes, including one condemning the newly emerging paper money system, are discussion between Fax and Forester on various aspects of the age's manners and morals. Seemingly only when they have exhausted Peacock's satiric syllabus do they manage to locate and rescue Anthelia in the final chapter. The culprits having been administered a strong dose of Sir Oran's natural justice, the novel concludes with the obligatory marriage of Forester and Anthelia (although the reader may wonder if Sir Oran is not more deserving of Anthelia's gratitude than his didactic guardian).

The literature of engagement. *Melincourt* was written during a period of social and political conservatism that spanned the first three decades of the nineteenth century. Liberals had still not recovered the confidence lost in the disillusioning wake of the French Revolution in the 1790s, while their unpatriotic (as it seemed to conservatives) opposition to British involvement in the Napoleonic Wars had further damaged their credibility. With Britain's victory in 1815, and the external threat removed, conservatives were nevertheless alarmed at mounting protest and violence at home on the part of unemployed laborers and tradesmen pressing for relief from economic hardship. Fear of possible revolution entrenched conservative attitudes among the propertied and mercantile classes, and the Tory government resorted to a number of alarmist measures, in 1817 suspending habeas corpus and passing a Seditious Meetings Bill. In the midst of this reactionary mood liberals felt beleaguered and defensive.

Melincourt reflects the ideological polarities of its age, for the battle lines are clearly drawn in this work. On one side are the reformers, those like Mr. Forester and Anthelia who are dissatisfied with society as it is, and desire to change it. On the other side are the reactionaries, who cling to tradition and oppose change of any kind. Peacock's own allegiances, in this his most explicitly partisan satire, are with the reformers. It is fitting that a pamphlet by Shelley entitled *A Proposal for Putting Reform to the Vote* should have appeared within a few weeks of *Melincourt*'s publication, for Shelley's influence has left an indelible imprint on *Melincourt*. If in 1813 Shelley found Peacock to be "not very ardent, nor his views very comprehensive," by 1816 he considered the author of *Melincourt* to be "an enemy to every shape of tyranny & superstitious imposture."

Shelley's somewhat mercurial affections aside, the notion that Peacock's opinions and attitudes had undergone a radical transition is borne out by *Melincourt* itself. The liberal thesis of this work stands in stark contrast to the "Hail Britannia" sentiments of *The Genius of the Thames,* which had so irritated Shelley just a few years earlier. There are of course many points of resemblance between Shelley and the proselytizing Mr. Forester of *Melincourt,* but Peacock is indebted to his friend for more than just a character in his novel. Association with Shelley helped Peacock to clarify his role as a writer in relation to his age and society. In the *Genius of the Thames* he had chosen the complacent role of panegyrist; in *Melincourt* he chooses the uncompromising role of social and political satirist.

Melincourt, more than any work Peacock had written or would write, urges emphatically the importance of engagement. As Mr. Fax says of an apathetic citizen he has just encountered, "There are many such, who think they have no business with politics: but they find to their cost that politics will have business with them" (2:325). Engagement, social and political, is the motivating principle in the ideal lover envisaged by Anthelia, who should combine the personal faithfulness of the lover with the public commitment of the reformer. Mr. Forester, in whom Anthelia will presently realize her ideal, defines this principle of engagement in typically uncompromising terms:

In every mode of human action there are two ways to be pursued—a good and a bad one. It is the duty of every man to ascertain the former, as clearly as his capacity will admit, by an accurate examination of general relations; and to act upon it rigidly, without regard to his own previous habits, or the common practice of the world. (2:50)

At the root of this philosophy is the "influence of personal example," as Forester admonishes his good-natured but complacent friend Sir Telegraph Paxarett. Futile though it may seem for the individual to pursue a cause in the face of general apathy or hostility, there is nevertheless much to be gained in the long term. Enough such instances of individual commitment will eventually turn the tide of custom and prejudice. Rejoicing at the success of the Anti-Saccharine Fête in chapter 27, Forester describes the resulting "efficacy of associated sympathies," using Shelley's favorite metaphor of the avalanche: "It is but to give an impulse of co-operation to any good and generous feeling, and its progressive accumulation, like that of an Alpine avalanche, though but a snow-ball at the summit, becomes a mountain in the valley" (2:299).

The fruitful engagement of the modern writer with society is *Melincourt*'s specific theme. "If he produce but a single volume consecrated to moral truth," as Mr. Forester admonishes Robert Southey's caricature Mr. Feathernest, "its effect must be good as far as it goes" (2:187–88). With the possible exception of the earlier *Sir Proteus, Melincourt* contains Peacock's harshest criticism of the Lake Poets and their alleged political apostasy. Wordsworth's long poem, *The Excursion* (1814), was seen by young liberals like Peacock and Shelley as a conservative affirmation of church and state, and thus proof of the elder writer's abnegation of his youthful ideals. In chapter 37 Fax and Forester outline the harmful consequences of such a retreat in their general condemnation of the Lake Poets:

We have seen a little horde of poets, who brought hither from the vales of the south, the harps which they had consecrated to Truth and Liberty, to acquire new energy in the mountain-winds: and now those harps are attuned to the praise of luxurious power, to the strains of courtly syco-phancy, and to the hymns of exploded superstition. (2:386).

In the episode that soon follows Fax and Forester are brought face to face with this very "horde" at Mainchance Villa in chapter 39. Peacock's satire in this episode is rather heavy-handed, and Mr.

Forester is predictably successful in demolishing the apostate poets
with his usual argumentative rigor. It is in the subsequent chapter,
when Forester plaintively wonders aloud "where then is the poet?"
(2:431), that is, the genuine poet, that perhaps we glimpse something of Peacock's personal struggle with this question.

Thus Peacock is anything but sanguine about the state of letters
in the present age, if his portrait of the venal "criticopoetical council"
gathered at Mainchance Villa is any indication. Indeed, the only
other author portrayed in *Melincourt* is a failed one. Desmond, who
is the subject of a story related to Forester by Mr. Fax in chapter
13, had come to London with the intention of applying his literary
talent for mankind's betterment. He was quickly disillusioned, however, upon finding the London literary world to be composed solely
by the likes of Messrs. Vamp and Foolscap, "the paragraph-mongers
of prostituted journals, the hireling compounders of party praise
and censure" (2:144). Ironically, Peacock himself would be the
recipient of both "party praise and censure" with the publication
of *Melincourt*. It is difficult not to see in the tale of the unfortunate
Desmond a parable of the young liberal writer cast adrift in an age
of cynicism and venality.

Past and present. *Melincourt* presents, besides Anthelia's and
Forester's idealistic notions of chivalry, other forms of veneration
for a feudal past that are much less idealistic. "The feudal spirit,"
warned William Godwin, "still survives that reduced the great mass
of mankind to the rank of slaves and cattle for the service of a few."[8]
Hence the regressive agenda outlined by the "criticopoetical council"
at Mainchance Villa:

> MR. KILLTHEDEAD.
> To make a stand against popular encroachment—
> MR. FEATHERNEST.
> To bring back the glorious ignorance of the feudal ages—
> MR. PAPERSTAMP.
> To rebuild the mystic temples of venerable superstition—
> MR. VAMP.
> To extinguish, totally, and finally, the light of the
> human understanding—   (2:417)

It is an agenda based solely on reactionary alarm: "We are all upon
gunpowder! The insane and the desperate are scattering firebrands!"
(2:409). Ironically, Peacock has taken for his text in this episode

an actual article from the *Quarterly Review* of 1816 (probably written by Southey) attacking what it called the "no-reasoners in favour of parliamentary reform."[9] The farce is much heightened at Mainchance Villa of course, but Peacock stays remarkably close to his source nevertheless.

The *Quarterly Review* article bases its case against reform on Edmund Burke's defense of the English constitution as something of organic growth evolved gradually over the centuries, and as such not to be tampered with by rationalizing reformers. The constitution is not "the creature of theory," the *Quarterly* argues; "it has grown with our growth, and been gradually modified by the changes through which society is always passing in its progress."[10] In *Melincourt* Peacock takes Burke's organic gradualism to its reductio ad absurdum.

The established order in *Melincourt* is indeed a living organism, but it breeds only corruption. Its roots, to use Burke's favorite image of the great tree, are "the wide-spreading roots of superstition and political imposture" (2:131), and the parasites it supports "insatiable accumulators, overgrown capitalists, fatteners on public spoil" (2:430). Lord Anophel Achthar takes his name from the Greek ("useless cumber of the ground"), while his father, Marquis of Agaric, seems to have derived his from a genus in botany ("agaricus . . . comprehending the mushroom, and a copious variety of toadstools" [2:80n.]) Representing the landed gentry are Mr. Lawrence Litigate of Muckwormsby Manor, Mr. Killthedead of Frogmarsh Hall, and Mr. Harum O'Scarum, Esq., proprietor of a "vast tract of undrained bog" (2:83). Others, of the commercial and professional middle classes and the clergy, include Richard Ratstail, Mr. Greenmould, Mr. Dross, and the Reverend Mr. Grovelgrub. All these characters, "excrescences on the body politic, typical of the disease and prophetic of decay" (2:430), embody collectively the established order, that pullulating mass of corruption, which, as one character puts it, "estimates conscience and Stilton cheese by the same criterion"— namely, by their rottenness (2:138).

As well as travestying Burkean organicism, Peacock exposes the rationale behind it. According to Southey's *Quarterly Review* article, "a people who are ignorant and know themselves to be so, will often judge rightly when they are called upon to think at all."[11] Hence the reactionaries at Mainchance Villa plot to bring back the "glorious ignorance of the feudal ages." Indeed, pressed to argue their position, *Melincourt*'s Tories frequently take refuge in doubtful metaphysics or just plain irrationalism. When he is cornered on a certain point in chapter 8, Mr. Feathernest (Southey) replies with "a volley of ponderous jargon" he has picked up from his friend Moley Mystic (2:86); responding to a reasonable request from Mr. Forester that he prove an assertion, Gifford's caricature, Mr. Vamp, exclaims: "Prove it! The editor of the Legitimate Review required to prove an assertion!" (2:401).

Despite their aggressive irrationalism, though, *Melincourt's* Tories are remarkably amenable to enlightened self-interest when it suits them to be. Burke's mystical definition of "things as they are" is fine as far as it goes, but as one very orthodox churchman informs Fax and Forester, "the present order of things I have made up my mind to stick by precisely as long as it lasts" (2:321). In chapter 9 ("The Philosophy of Ballads") Walter Scott's caricature, Mr. Derrydown, demonstrates "the truth of things" as it is to be found in an ancient ballad. The result is a cynical discourse on "love and prudence"—he even endorses Malthusianism at one point!—a justification of "prudential reasoning" on the authority of primitive poetry (2:94).

Melincourt's reactionaries, then, appeal to the past in order to justify the abuses of the present. They wish to keep intact "the great feudal fortress of society" (2:150) by keeping the populace in the thralls of ignorance and superstition. The consequences of such a program are ominously hinted at throughout the novel. Although the French Revolution is mentioned only once (2:119), its ghost hovers uneasily over *Melincourt's* pages alongside "the Ghost of Feudal Times" invoked by Moley Mystic and his ilk. The Shelleyan tempest, which overcomes a peaceful mountain valley through which Anthelia wanders in chapter 10 ("The Torrent"), is, with its "energies of liberty and power" (2:104), a portent and a warning. The failure of a country bank engenders a dangerously ugly mood in a mob of ruined depositors who gather in chapter 30 ("The Paper Mill"). A riot that levels the "ancient and venerable borough of Onevote" (rebuilt, ironically, a few days afterwards) at the end of chapter 22 is even more obvious in its political implications, as is the sudden explosion that rousts the reactionary Moley Mystic from his bedchambers in chapter 31.

Melincourt's reformers, by contrast, are concerned with the living spirit, rather than the dead letter, of the past. Their aim is not to destroy the present order, any more than it is to clutch blindly onto its every archaic feature out of a misguided (or exploitive) regard for tradition. Rather, they demonstrate reforming aims dedicated to adapting the best of the past to the best of the present. The quasi-feudal agrarian community established on Forester's estate recalls "images of better times" (2:287)—as Forester informs another character, "I seek no more than I know to have existed" (2:116)—but it represents a reforming program as well, pointedly distinguished from the reactionary program of *Melincourt*'s Tories. Melincourt Castle illustrates palpably this spirit of synthesis in its very structure, for "while one half of the edifice was fast improving into a picturesque ruin, the other was as rapidly degenerating, in its interior at least, into a comfortable modern dwelling" (2:8–9). Forester's habitation, Redrose Abbey, seems to have undergone a similar process, and, fittingly, Sir Telegraph observes its resemblance to Melincourt Castle (2:33).

It is the owner of Redrose Abbey, however, who most nearly approaches this ideal synthesis of the best of past and present. Mr. Forester combines the knightly virtues of courage and honor with the enlightened social views of a nineteenth-century reformer. In rescuing Anthelia from the obnoxious Lord Achthar he shows himself in the former capacity, while in his reforming zeal he demonstrates his fealty to the "greatest happiness." It is Forester who confirms Anthelia's belief that it is possible "to find as true a knight-errant in a brown coat in the nineteenth century, as in a suit of golden armour in the days of Charlemagne" (2:24). Past and present are reconciled, and the spirits of chivalry and liberalism become one. It was, significantly, "such a rare combination of an enthusiasm almost chivalrous for the liberty and happiness of mankind, with a calm philosophical judgment," that Peacock praised in the real-life reformer Thomas Jefferson (9:185).

Nightmare Abbey (1818)

In a series of letters written between May and September 1818 Peacock informed his friend Shelley, now in Italy, of the English weather, of the current political and literary news, and, it probably seemed to Shelley, rather perfunctorily of a novel-in-progress, *Nightmare Abbey*. Indeed, Shelley was evidently not clear on the nature and object of Peacock's newest satire. Upon hearing that the work in question had been completed, he wrote to congratulate the author, and fell into the zealous strain that characterizes *Nightmare Abbey*'s hero and, as it turned out, Shelley's satiric portrait, Scythrop Glowry. "I hope that you have given the enemy no quarter. Remember, it is a sacred war," he admonished Peacock. [12]

In a subsequent letter Peacock attempted to clarify for his friend the nature of his newest satire. "I thought I had fully explained to you the object of *Nightmare Abbey*," he writes, "which was merely to bring to a sort of philosophical focus a few of the morbidities of modern literature, and to let in a little daylight on its atrabilarious [*sic*] complexion" (8:204). This object was clear enough to Shelley when he read the novel. Although perhaps somewhat taken aback by what was so obviously a caricature of his own life and opinions, he accepted it in good humor, and, in Peacock's words, "took to himself the character of Scythrop" (8:497n.).

Shelley, of course, had a bias, which was clearly reflected in his partiality to the earlier *Melincourt*. There, with the Shelley-like Sylvan Forester as his mouthpiece, Peacock had taken an unequivocal stand against superstition and tyranny. The author of *Nightmare Abbey*, however, does not wear his politics on his sleeve, although perhaps "more of the true spirit," albeit in comically distorted form, remains in this work than Shelley was able or willing to see. The difference is that whereas *Melincourt*'s Mr. Forester is not intended as a satiric butt, *Nightmare Abbey*'s Scythrop Glowry is rarely anything else. Whereas Forester's political views, reflecting the views of Shelley and Peacock at this time, are to be taken at face value, it is impossible to take seriously very much of Scythrop's creed, characterized as it is by excessive zeal and a heavy underscoring of melodrama.

Perhaps the best-loved of Peacock's novels today, *Nightmare Abbey* received surprisingly little notice when it first appeared. *Blackwood's Magazine* noted it in a list of new publications for November 1818, while the following month it received a rather neutral review in the *Literary Gazette*. The *Monthly Review*, however, expressed delight at *Nightmare Abbey*'s send-up of "the gloomy philosophy and metaphysical poetry of the present day" (1:lxxxiv). A contemporary of Peacock's, the discerning Mary Mitford, read the novel and described it in a letter to a friend:

I have been laughing at *Nightmare Abbey,* the pleasantest of all Mr. Peacock's works, whether in verse or prose, *Rhodo-daphne* and *Melincourt* included.

I have not met with a more cheerful or amiable piece of *raillerie*. The chief objects of his attack are misanthropical poetry and transcendental metaphysics (deuce take Mr. Peacock for putting me [to] such hard words) in the persons of Lord Byron and my poor dear friend Mr. Coleridge—the last in particular fares most lamentably. (1:lxxxiv)

It is not known how Coleridge reacted to this his third lampooning by Peacock; Byron, for his part, sent the author a rosebud in appreciation.

Nightmare Abbey invites contrasts with the novel directly preceding it. Predominantly a literary satire, it does not plunge into the hurly-burly of contemporary social controversy as *Melincourt* does, nor square off nearly so obviously on matters of political ideology. Nevertheless, it analyzes the characteristic spirit of the age in politics and manners, as well as in literature.

Melodrama and comedy. *Nightmare Abbey* signals a return to the style of *Headlong Hall*. It has the same brevity and wit, the same skeptical detachment that characterizes Peacock at his best. Gone is the loose episodic structure of *Melincourt,* replaced by a more complicated, yet compact, plot. The dialogue is witty and, an advance over both earlier novels, suited to the individual speakers. Finally, it returns to the simple and typically Peacockian device of a country house filled with eccentric guests.

This particular country house, indeed, is well suited to the novel's theme. Nightmare Abbey is "a venerable family-mansion, in a highly picturesque state of semidilapidation, pleasantly situated on a strip of dry land between the sea and the fens, at the verge of the county of Lincoln" (3:1). "Pleasantly situated" should be taken advisedly, for this phrase reflects a system of aesthetic and moral values that is seriously askew. Christopher Glowry, Esq., Nightmare Abbey's proprietor, combines the roles of host and crotcheteer, selecting his servants and guests alike on the basis of his naturally "atrabilarious [*sic*] temperament" (3:1). One favored visitor, indeed, Mr. Flosky, is a very morbid gentleman whose "very fine sense of the grim and the tearful" (3:9) highly recommends him to the lachrymose Mr. Glowry. Yet another caricature of Coleridge, Flosky involves himself in "transcendental darkness" like Moley Mystic in *Melincourt* and is the sworn enemy of common sense. However, where Mr. Mystic represents the views of Coleridge the political thinker, Flosky is conceived along the lines of Coleridge the literary theorist. Like the latter, he discourses on the distinction between fancy and imagination, having "written seven hundred pages of promise to elucidate it" (3:75), and in chapter 8 describes a poem composed by him in his sleep which is probably "Kubla Khan."

Another visitor at Nightmare Abbey is Mr. Toobad "the Manichaean Millenarian," whose name sufficiently explains why he is Mr. Glowry's most welcome guest. Based in part on the eccentric J. F. Newton of Bracknell, Mr. Toobad holds the Manichaean belief that the world is ruled alternately by a good principle and an evil principle; needless to say, he is convinced that the evil principle is currently in the ascendent, and will continue to be for some time to come. Less welcome at Nightmare Abbey, by contrast, is the cheerful Mr. Hilary whom family obligations compel Mr. Glowry to suffer as an occasional guest.

Other guests who turn up during the course of the novel include: Reverend Larnyx, who, as his name suggests, is mainly a voice and a gullet like his clerical predecessors in the other novels; Mr. Asterias, an indefatigable and cheerful ichthyologist, who is convinced of the existence of mermaids; and a gentleman of fashion named Mr. Listless whose languid manners and intellect embody for Peacock the enervated tastes of the reading public. Lord Byron makes a memorable appearance as Mr. Cypress the poet in chapter 11. Mr. Cypress "has quarrelled with his wife," and in consequence is disillusioned with humanity (3:103). All these characters, cheerful and gloomy alike, enjoy the hospitality of Nightmare Abbey and engage in lively debate behind its crumbling, ivy-coverd walls.

When the novel opens, Mr. Glowry's only son and heir, Scythrop, has suffered a disappointment in love. After pledging eternal love, he and one Miss Emily Girouette have been torn asunder by parental interests (recalling perhaps the similar termination of Shelley's engagement to Harriet Grove in 1810). Disillusioned, Scythrop secludes himself in his tower at Nightmare Abbey, where he devours German tragedies and ponderous tomes of transcendental philosophy. He becomes infected with a *"passion for reforming the world"* (3:14), writing radical pamphlets and dreaming of secret societies dedicated to the regeneration of mankind. Again, this curious blend of Gothic romance and radicalism recalls the youthful Shelley, the "votary of romance" who became the disciple of William Godwin.

A love triangle forms the basis of *Nightmare Abbey*'s plot. Even as Scythrop enacts Gothic fantasies in his tower, Miss Marionetta

Celestina O'Carroll has arrived at Nightmare Abbey with her uncle Mr. Hilary. Marionetta is a lively and sensible young woman, and also something of a flirt. In no time, Scythrop has forgotten his reforming schemes and fallen in love with her. But the course of true love never runs smooth in Peacock. Mr. Glowry, Sr. and Mr. Toobad have, against the wishes of their children, agreed on an arranged marriage between Scythrop and Mr. Toobad's daughter Celinda, who, unlike Marionetta, is blessed with a gloomy temperament and an ample fortune. That young lady, however, is of an independent turn of mind and flees her father's house in order to protest this abuse of parental prerogative. By a strange coincidence, she appears one evening in Scythrop's tower under the pseudonym of Stella. Captivated by this lady's air of mystery, Scythrop, who is unaware of her true identity, agrees to shelter her from the "atrocious persecution" from which she is fleeing (3:93). Stella, significantly, is Marionetta's temperamental opposite, being serious and passionate, where Marionetta is frivolous and sensible.

The susceptible Scythrop now finds himself in a dilemma, caught between his infatuation for both ladies. Shelley had himself been involved in a similar situation four years before, which was anything but comic in its circumstances. Already married to Harriet Shelley, on whom Peacock is said to have based Marionetta, Shelley became attracted to Mary Godwin, whose serious, intellectual nature has been identified with that of Celinda Toobad. In 1814 Shelley and Mary eloped, marrying two years later following Harriet's suicide in 1816. It is difficult to ignore the parallel in Peacock's novel; the question of its propriety is a ticklish one, although Shelley himself does not seem to have been offended.

Of course, the fictional situation develops along far less tragic lines. When Marionetta and Celinda discover each other in chapter 13, both ladies leave Nightmare Abbey in a state of high indignation, eventually to find other husbands. Left high and dry, Scythrop resolves on the dramatic course of suicide, but at the novel's end settles for a bottle of Madeira instead. *Nightmare Abbey* is the only one of Peacock's novels in which the hero does not marry; yet this violation of comic convention notwithstanding, *Nightmare Abbey* is Peacock's most emphatic affirmation of the comic spirit.

Anatomy of black bile.   "The fourth canto of *Childe Harold* is really too bad," Peacock complained in one of his letters to Shelley. "I cannot consent to be *auditor tantum* of this systematical 'poisoning' of the 'mind' of the 'reading public' " (8:193). What Peacock objected to in Byron's poem and works like it, was a spirit of misanthropy and despair, which he though socially devitalizing. This was something of a reverse for the author of *Palmyra* and *The Philosophy of Melancholy,* who had trod very much the same ground as the gloomy Childe ("Short is the space to man assign'd / This earthly vale to tread" [6:18]). Indeed, Peacock's abrupt volte-face from romantic versifier to comic-satiric novelist is perhaps most dramatically illustrated in *Nightmare Abbey,* which is among other things an explicit statement of literary orientation. Faced with what he believed to be an unhealthy tendency in contemporary literature, Peacock found it necessary in this work "to 'make a stand' against the 'encroachments' of black bile" (8:193). He would, of course, make his stand from the clear vantage ground of comedy.

As much as the unfinished "Essay on Fashionable Literature," which Peacock began the same year, *Nightmare Abbey* anatomizes the popular literature of the day. In chapter 5 a parcel of books arrives for Mr. Listless, and Mr. Flosky enumerates the contents:

(*Turning over the leaves.*) " 'Devilman, a novel.' Hm. Hatred—revenge—misanthropy—and quotations from the Bible. Hm. This is the morbid anatomy of black bile.—'Paul Jones, a poem.' Hm. I see how it is. Paul Jones, an amiable enthusiast—disappointed in his affections—turns pirate from ennui and magnanimity—cuts various masculine throats, wins various feminine hearts—is hanged at the yard-arm! The catastrophe is very awkward, and very unpoetical." (3:39)

The poem, "Paul Jones," could refer to any one of Byron's popular oriental tales, which had for their heroes scoundrels of the type outlined above. "Devilman" specifically refers to *Mandeville,* a novel by William Godwin that had appeared in 1817. After he had read it, Shelley wrote to Godwin, "we wonder whence you drew the darkness with which its shades are deepened until the epithet of tenfold night almost ceases to be a metaphor."[13]

Mr. Flosky, however, does not wonder at the source of "Devilman's" gloom. He matter-of-factly attributes it to a peevish humor of the age, and thus of a kind with the "blue devils" that plague the neurotic Mr. Glowry. But it is this very quality that recommends such literary productions to Mr. Listless, whose fashionable tastes are a reliable guide to those of the reading public at large. "Modern books are very consolatory and congenial to my feelings," points out this character. "There is, as it were, a delightful northeast wind, an intellectual blight breathing through them; a delicious misanthropy and discontent, that demonstrates the nullity of virtue and energy, and puts me in good humour with myself and my sofa" (3:41). What this literature of gloom and despair offers is not a criticism of life but merely a rationalization of self-indulgence, moral and emotional. As Mr. Listless says elsewhere in reply to a critical interlocutor, it "reconciles me to my favourite pursuit of doing nothing, by showing me that nobody is worth doing any thing for" (3:67).

The deleterious effects of this "intellectual blight" are everywhere present in *Nightmare Abbey,* but nowhere so much as in the figure of Scythrop Glowry. "A gloomy brow and a tragical voice seem to have been of late the characteristics of fashionable manners," Mr. Asterias observes (3:65), and he might be describing the young scion of Nightmare Abbey.

Scythrop exhibits in all he says and does an inability to distinguish between life and literature, which is a consequence of the morbid self-indulgence sanctioned by Mr. Listless and the age: "In the congenial solitude of Nightmare Abbey, the distempered ideas of metaphysical romance and romantic metaphysics had ample time and space to germinate into a fertile crop of chimeras, which rapidly shot up into vigorous and abundant vegetation" (3:14). He sleeps with *Horrid Mysteries* under his pillow and passes his days stalking Nightmare Abbey like a melodramatic Gothic villain. In chapter 3 Marionetta happens upon him during one of his reveries, and in the exchange that follows Scythrop has clearly taken a page from Gothic literature. "Let us each open a vein in the other's arm," he implores his astonished sweetheart, "mix our blood in a bowl, and drink it as a sacrament of love" (3:24). Marionetta has not the stomach for such romantic pledges, however, and flees her high-wrought suitor.

Celinda Toobad, by contrast, is altogether a more suitable subject for Scythrop. Celinda has taken the pseudonym "Stella" from Goethe's work of that name, and her mysterious appearance at Scythrop's tower is compared to that of the sinister Geraldine in Coleridge's *Christabel* (3:89). Moreover, she embodies the curious combination of Gothic melodrama and radical politics that characterizes Scythrop's enthusiasms:

She had a lively sense of all the oppressions that are done under the sun; and the vivid pictures which her imagination presented to her of the numberless scenes of injustice and misery which are being acted at every moment in every part of the inhabited world, gave an habitual seriousness to her physiognomy, that made it seem as if a smile had never once hovered on her lips. She was intimately conversant with the German language and literature; and Scythrop listened with delight to her repetitions of her favourite passages from Schiller and Göethe. (3:93–94)

It is easy to see how this character has come to be identified with Shelley's second wife Mary, the daughter of William Godwin and Mary Wollstonecraft, and the author of *Frankenstein.*

Scythrop, for his part, clearly shares Shelley's own penchant for self-dramatization, which Peacock would describe in his memoirs of Shelley (8:103).[14] Indeed, if the triangle depicted in *Nightmare Abbey* unavoidably recalls the real-life Shelley-Harriet-Mary episode, it appears to owe a debt as well to Göethe's *Stella,* which also depicts such a situation. Similarly, just as Shelley, like Scythrop, at least considered suicide as a solution to his dilemma ("Memoirs," 8:91), so, by coincidence, does the hero of *The Sorrows of Werter,* another work by Göethe often in Scythrop's hand.

Nightmare Abbey is something more than art imitating life imitating art, however. Scythrop's choice between the gloomy Stella and the sprightly Marionetta is also a choice between Thalia and Melpomene (3:33), between comedy and tragedy. As determined as Scythrop may be to give his situation a tragical coloring, comic circumstances conspire against him. The scene in which Stella and Marionetta discover each other in chapter 13 reads like the denouement of a stage-comedy—Sheridan's *School for Scandal,* to be precise.[15] Shelley and Peacock had in fact attended a performance of this play together, and Shelley had strongly disapproved, according to Peacock's account in the "Memoirs." "I see the purpose of this comedy," he had claimed. "It is to associate virtue with bottles and glasses, and villany [*sic*] with books" (8:81). Peacock promotes no such philistine notions in *Nightmare Abbey,* of course, but when Scythrop chooses the bottle over the pistol at this novel's end, one particular class of books, the literature of gloom, is surely condemned as villainous in its influence.

The politics of despair.   The dominant note in *Nightmare Abbey* is disappointment—in love and in politics. There is much in Scythrop's and Stella's political enthusiasms of the spirit of the 1790s, which the younger romantics, Shelley in particular, were attempting to revive. There is also much of the disappointment that, following the revolutionary decade, caused many, including older romantics like Wordsworth and Coleridge, to disavow the radical ideals of their youth. In his preface to *The Revolt of Islam,* published the same year as *Nightmare Abbey,* Shelley describes these poles of sentiment, "at first the sanguine eagerness for good" engendered by the French Revolution, then the disillusionment that followed "the first reverses of hope."[16]

A key figure in Peacock's treatment of this theme in *Nightmare Abbey* is Mr. Flosky. Like Coleridge, on whom he is based, Flosky is a political apostate—formerly a zealous young radical, now as a consequence of his disappointments in politics, a Tory of particularly reactionary views:

He had been in his youth an enthusiast for liberty, and had hailed the dawn of the French Revolution as the promise of a day that was to banish war and slavery, and every form of vice and misery, from the face of the earth. Because all this was not done, he deduced that nothing was done; and from this deduction, according to his system of logic, he drew a conclusion that worse than nothing was done; that the overthrow of the feudal fortresses of tyranny and superstition was the greatest calamity that had ever befallen mankind; and that their only hope now was to rake the rubbish together, and rebuild it without any of those loopholes by which the light had originally crept in. (3:10)

At first glance, this seems to be another tirade against "tyranny and superstition" of the kind that characterizes *Melincourt.* And yet Peacock is equally critical of the radical program here. Flosky's youthful expectations as an "enthusiast for liberty" seem to have been as excessive as his conservative views are at present. Indeed, his abrupt transition from radical to reactionary is the inevitable consequence of disappointed, because unrealistic, enthusiasm.

Mary Shelley once said that her husband "had been from youth the victim of the state of feeling inspired by the reaction of the French Revolution."[17] Such a "state of feeling" seems to underlie Peacock's characterization of Scythrop Glowry, who, more than just caricaturing Shelley, virtually embodies the postrevolutionary generation and their mood. *Nightmare Abbey* opens, we recall, to find Scythrop's "sensitive spirit" badly bruised after his breakup with Miss Girouette (3:5), whose name (French for weathercock) is some indication of the future hopes and disappointments in store for him.

Like Mr. Flosky after the shattering of his youthful idealism, Scythrop becomes disillusioned with humanity and shuts himself up in his tower, where he somehow becomes an enthusiast for liberty. Thereafter, his hopes and disappointments in both love and politics are Peacock's main theme.

For Howard Mills, Scythrop represents the dangers of "the intensely personal."[18] This apt observation might be extended to include many of *Nightmare Abbey's* other characters, for the postrevolutionary mood informing the novel is a queer jumble of personal and. philosophical complaints. One of *Nightmare Abbey's* mottoes, "There's a dark lantern of the spirit, / Which none see by but those who bear it," is taken from the seventeenth-century satirist Samuel Butler and sets the tone for what follows. In chapter 1, for example, we learn that the late Mrs. Glowry, who was apparently as unhappy in marriage as her husband, "laid on external things the blame of her mind's internal disorder, and thus became by degrees an accomplished scold" (3:2). Mr. Glowry's habitual pessimism is likewise the result of personal disappointments—Mrs. Glowry among them—but this has not stopped him from projecting his gloom onto the world at large and turning Nightmare Abbey into a salon for political and moral misanthropes of every kind. One of these latter indeed, the Byronic Mr. Cypress, denies all responsibility to mankind because he has quarrelled with his wife (3:103). The radical Stella is "an enthusiast in subjects of general interest" (3:98); yet her abstract rhetoric is somewhat undercut by the sole cause of her discontent, a domineering father. Such comic incongruities run through the novel, but Peacock's send-up of postrevolutionary despair is most succinctly expressed in Mr. Flosky's attribution of the age's ills to "tea, late dinners, and the French Revolution" (3:48).

The ideological battle lines in *Nightmare Abbey* are not nearly as clear-cut as they are in *Melincourt*. If the latter work pits radicals against reactionaries in a kind of "sacred war," to use Shelley's phrase, *Nightmare Abbey* pits common sense against enthusiasm. Party allegiances, as such, are not a factor in *Nightmare Abbey,* for it is not apparent just who constitutes the forces of light and who the forces of darkness here. Indeed, radicals and reactionaries seem to have joined forces insofar as they are alike viewed by Peacock as negative, regressive forces, irrespective of ideology. Hence one of the marriages with which the novel concludes is between the radical Stella and the reactionary Mr. Mystic, who, their differing political creeds notwithstanding, are of a kind. According to the sanguine Mr. Hilary, they and the other misguided enthusiasts in the novel are together engaged in "a conspiracy against cheerfulness" (3:110). Mr. Hilary argues that "the highest wisdom and the highest genius have been invariably accompanied with cheerfulness," and that the proper response to disappointment is not to rail at man and the world for being imperfect, but "to reconcile man as he is to the world as it is, to preserve and improve all that is good, and destroy or alleviate all that is evil" (3:109).

Enthusiasm is not proscribed utterly in *Nightmare Abbey,* though, for there is one enthusiast in the novel who seems to enjoy Peacock's sanction. Mr. Asterias, the ichthyologist, is the active exponent of Mr. Hilary's "spirit and science" of cheerfulness. Where Hilary rebukes the morbid turn taken by the age's "speculative" energies, Mr. Asterias puts to shame the age's squandering of its "active" energies in such figures as Byron's Childe Harold by the example of his own wide-ranging and fearless expeditions in pursuit of scientific knowledge. Asterias is, it is true, a typical Peacockian crotcheteer in terms of his obsession with finding a genuine mermaid, but in this case the idée fixe offers stability against the extreme fluctuations of spirit to which Scythrop and his contemporaries are subject. Mr. Asterias has looked in vain for his mermaid, "and reaped disappointment, but not despair" (3:58).

Nightmare Abbey evinces a saving detachment from the Shelleyan strain so dominant in *Melincourt.* Perhaps it was also a hard-won detachment, for Shelley's zeal must have been very infectious to have won over the "cold scholar" whom Mrs. J. F. Newton observed laughing at the eccentric little circle at Bracknell. Peacock wrote *Nightmare Abbey* only after Shelley's departure to Italy, and throughout his correspondence with Shelley during this period he was curiously diffident about this work, for which Shelley chided him.[19] And yet if Peacock seems to eschew the emphatic political commitment of *Melincourt* in his third novel, *Nightmare Abbey* does not by any means signal a retreat from fruitful social engagement. As his letters to Peacock indicate, Shelley saw in "the misdirected enthusiasm of Scythrop what J[esus] C[hrist] calls the salt of the earth."[20] Peacock, it is certain, recognized this quality in his friend

and in all enthusiasts like him. *Nightmare Abbey* is not a disavowal
of the *"passion for reforming the world,"* but a comic corrective aimed
at the excesses to which this passion, if not balanced by common
sense, can lead.

Chapter Five
Crotchet Castle and *Gryll Grange:* The Mature Voice

In the decade following the publication of *Nightmare Abbey*, Peacock's life underwent a number of changes, personal and professional. He had married Jane Gryffydh in 1820 and settled into his house at Lower Halliford to raise a family. Shelley had died in 1822, and in 1819 Peacock had taken up his post at the East India Company, where he came into contact with a circle of utilitarian thinkers including Jeremy Bentham, James Mill, and John Stuart Mill. Personal and professional duties permitting, Peacock kept his hand in as a writer. His two satiric romances, *Maid Marian* (1822) and *The Misfortunes of Elphin* (1829), were published during this period, and will be considered in the next chapter. As a result of his acquaintance with the utilitarians at the India House, Peacock also became a contributor to the utilitarian *Westminister Review,* in which several of his essays appeared. One further product of Peacock's association with the leading liberal thinkers of the day was *Crotchet Castle,* published in 1831.

Crotchet Castle (1831)

Separated by some dozen years from the earlier novels of talk, *Crotchet Castle* is something of a watershed for Peacock. If his earlier works, including the two satiric romances, had been liberal in their sympathies, *Crotchet Castle,* as Marilyn Butler observes, "is a satire on a world in which liberalism has become orthodoxy."[1] Such a shift in allegiance, if only apparent, was not lost on contemporary readers. The *Westminster Review* expressed disappointment that "men are most inclined to satirise that of which they know the most"— alluding to Peacock's utilitarian acquaintances at the India House— and urged him to redirect his satire to "the greater nuisances which prey upon the well-being of society" (1:cli). Leigh Hunt's liberal *Examiner* was similarly disappointed in Peacock, observing that "his intentions of drollery seem to us generally abortive" (1:cli). By contrast, the more conservative *Literary Gazette* was delighted by *Crotchet Castle's* "palpable hits" and characterized the author as "the wittiest writer in England" (1:cl).

Modern reaction to the novel has been similarly divided.[2] Moreover, there is also the question of where Peacock himself stands on the many issues debated in *Crotchet Castle*—always a good question in Peacock, but one especially problematic here. The difficulty lies mainly in *Crotchet Castle's* wide frame of reference. Each of the three earlier novels of talk addresses itself to some specific issue that underlies even the most far-ranging of discussions. In *Headlong Hall* it is the idea of progress, which manifests itself in everything from phrenology to landscape design, while *Melincourt* and *Nightmare Abbey* concern themselves with politics and literature respectively, and if these concerns overlap constantly it is always with ultimate reference to the novel's main satiric focus. By contrast, *Crotchet Castle,* in Butler's words, "broadly and even amorphously directs itself to the subject of culture."[3] But the diffuseness is only apparent; through the medley of themes that crowd *Crotchet Castle* a coherent point of view can be discerned, faintly at times it is true, yet definite and in some ways definitive.

Love in a calculating age. *Crotchet Castle* gives in its first chapter a brief account of its host-character's genealogy. Unlike Squire Headlong, however, Ebenezer Mac Crotchet does not possess a very distinguished or long lineage. He has indeed no claims on his Thames valley estate and its castellated villa beyond those of strictly legal ownership and a spurious coat of arms. The son of a commercial adventurer from Scotland, he made his fortune in the "alley" (London's stock market), and is now a retired widower. Nevertheless, he is enough like Peacock's other hosts to crave the company of thinking men, "and being very hospitable in his establishment, and liberal in his invitations, a numerous detachment from the advanced guard of the 'march of intellect,' often marched down to Crotchet Castle" (4:6).

Mr. Crotchet's guests seem an ill-assorted group. There is the Reverend Doctor Folliot, whose prominence in the novel has led some to identify his views too closely with those of Peacock. Possessing a fund of classical learning and love of good food and wine, Folliot is also a rabid Tory, and his narrowness falls prey to Peacock's irony on occasion. Then there is Mr. Mac Quedy, an exponent of political economy, an enormously influential school of thought that treated all social and political issues in economic terms. One of Reverend Folliot's most prominent traits is the abhorrence in which he holds the views of Mr. Mac Quedy, who "turns all the affairs of this world into questions of buying and selling" (4:58). With their opposing views, Folliot and Mac Quedy figure in the foreground of *Crotchet Castle's* numerous debates. There are other voices, however, among them that of Mr. Toogood the cooperationalist. This character is based on Robert Owen, a contemporary industrialist and social reformer who established a factory known as New Lanark in which the factory hands lived and worked under his paternalistic sway. Another guest is Mr. Chainmail, a young antiquarian who venerates the Middle Ages to the extent that he and his household at Chainmail Hall live after the manner of the twelfth century.

A host of minor eccentrics also grace Mr. Crotchet's table. Mr. Skionar is the last of Peacock's Coleridgean caricatures, though he plays little part in the novel. Mr. Firedamp is convinced of the malarial properties of water, while Mr. Philpot is an enthusiast of rivers. Mr. Henbane is a toxicologist who demonstrates his science by poisoning cats, and Dr. Morobific is an early advocate of inoculation. Mr. Eavesdrop is a journalist who has made his name by exploiting his acquaintances in print. Much more amenable to Peacock's own tastes, we may be sure, is Mr. Trillo who believes that "the sole end of all enlightened society is to get up a good opera" (4:64).

Crotchet Castle opens on two broken romances. Mr. Crotchet's loan-jobbing, stockbroking son, Crotchet, Jr., had been about to increase his fortune by marrying the daughter of a great banker named Timothy Touchandgo who, just before that happy event was to have taken place, had to flee the country when his bank failed. As a result, the fortune that young Crotchet had intended to marry not forthcoming, "this tender affair of the heart was nipped in the bud" (4:8). The young lady in question, Susannah Touchandgo, has retired from the world and lives in rural seclusion in North Wales. Always with an eye to his advantage, however, Crotchet, Jr., is now engaged to Lady Clarinda, who is the daughter of a certain Lord Foolincourt, one of the old nobility who has fallen on hard financial times. Her brother Lord Bossnowl is similarly engaged to Crotchet, Jr.'s sister, whose name Lemma is Greek for profit or gain. What we have here, then, is a match between the old nobility, venerable and connected but swiftly declining, and an aggressive new mercantile class eager for social legitimacy.

Just as Crotchet, Jr., has coolly jilted his fiancée after her sudden reverse in fortune, so Clarinda seems to have broken off an "affair of the heart" (4:36) with the ardent, but poor, Captain Fitzchrome, and from motives no less mercenary. The "doctrines of worldly wisdom" (4:130) with which she repels Captain Fitzchrome's suit are as pragmatic as those of political economy and are drawn, moreover, from a familiar source. When the captain expresses his sorrow at her expedient philosophy, she replies:

"What, because I have made up my mind not to give away my heart when I can sell it? I will introduce you to my new acquaintance, Mr. Mac Quedy: he will talk to you by the hour about exchangeable value, and show you that no rational being will part with any thing, except to the highest bidder." (4:41)

Mr. Mac Quedy, Clarinda tells the captain, "has satisfied me that I am a commodity in the market, and that I ought to set myself at a high price. So you see he who would have me must bid for me" (4:58). It is never clear how serious the playful Clarinda is in what she says, but Captain Fitzchrome takes her at her word, and professes himself shocked at such sentiments. Love and marriage, indeed "all the affairs of this world," have been resolved into "questions of buying and selling" in this philosophy. Value ceases to have a moral or even an aesthetic basis: all is judged according to its market price. Peacock is describing on a personal level here what contemporary critics of political economy perceived in early nineteenth-century society as a whole. "Profit and loss became the rule of conduct," observed Robert Southey in 1829; "in came calculation, and out went feeling."[4]

It is significant that Captain Fitzchrome finally wins Lady Clarinda, but only at the novel's end during the Yuletide celebrations at Chainmail Hall. The process leading up to this reconciliation, if perhaps just a bit less contrived in terms of narrative than similar arrangements in Peacock, is nevertheless prepared for on an intellectual level. At Mr. Crotchet's modern castellated villa any sympathy between the captain and Clarinda is necessarily obstructed by the presiding commercial spirit of the place. Both Crotchet Castle and its owner are products of this spirit, calculating, rational, and closed off from the past, for all goes forward in "The March of Mind." Romance and sentiment are excluded here, as they are in that other closed system, political economy. However, once removed from this locality, the novel's action takes a very different course. In chapter 9 Mr. Crotchet brings his guests on a convivial Thames voyage, which takes us from the modern, calculating world represented by Crotchet Castle to the medieval setting of Oxford to, finally, the rustic countryside of North Wales, thus effecting a kind of voyage back in time.[5]

One of the party on this voyage, Mr. Chainmail, leaves the others in order to explore the scenery by himself, and chances to meet the reclusive Miss Touchandgo. The romance that develops between Mr. Chainmail and Miss Touchandgo in the idyllic Welsh setting of Merionethshire demonstrates the possibility of genuine love even in an age of calculation. Although he insists in a discussion with Captain Fitzchrome in chapter 12 that the present age is incapable of "the high impassioned love" of chivalry, Mr. Chainmail allows for the existence in modern man of certain "tastes and feelings" (4:145) that are amenable to that ideal of humane conduct so grievously lacking in a world of Crotchets and Mac Quedys. It is this pragmatism that enables Mr. Chainmail finally to overcome his own feudal prejudices about lineage when he learns the truth about Miss Touchandgo's mercantile background, for "she is," as he points out to the captain, "according to modern notions, a lady of gentle blood" (4:184). In conceding to modern mores to this extent, Mr. Chainmail is following both his reason and his feeling.

Clarinda, by contrast, has followed neither. By surrendering entirely to the calculating spirit of the age, and allowing herself to be led by Mr. Mac Quedy's cold precepts, she is in imminent danger of sacrificing her happiness for gain, just as Crotchet, Jr., had done when he rejected Susannah Touchandgo's love, "as the renegade tramples on the emblems of a faith which his interest only, and not his heart or his reason, has rejected" (4:163). When, at the novel's end, she follows her heart and accepts her true love, Captain Fitzchrome, she has taken the truly enlightened course. "Wiser were the lovers, / In the days of old" (4:210) are the concluding lines of the ballad that accompanies this reconciliation, and might be taken for the story's moral.

The dismal science. Lying behind the conflict of sentiment and calculation that informs the romantic intrigues of *Crotchet Castle* is the phenomenon of political economy, or the "dismal science," as its critics termed it. Political economy holds that a free and open market, through competition and the profit incentive, provides the most efficient means of creating and distributing wealth, and that influences external to the market, such as government and trade unions, only disrupt this natural economic order. The decades preceding *Crotchet Castle's* publication had witnessed the rapid ascent of political economy to a position of such authority that, to some at least, it seemed to offer an exact science of government and society. Hence Lady Clarinda's rather sweeping, and ironic, claims for Mr. Mac Quedy, "who lays down the law about every thing, and therefore may be taken to understand every thing" (4:57–58).

Mr. Mac Quedy is the chief apologist for the "pound-shilling-and-pence philosophy" (4:59) by which so many of *Crotchet Castle's* characters seem to live. He is preoccupied solely with such matters as "rent, profit, wages, and currency" (4:17), "exchangeable value" (4:44), and "the division of labour" (4:71). To his mastery of the "dismal science," moreover, he brings an Enlightenment historical perspective, for complementing his political economist's jargon is the language of the Scottish historians of the eighteenth century. Like the latter, Mac Quedy discourses on "the progress of civilisation" and compares savage man to polished man (4:26), stipulating "respect for property" as an essential condition for the "perfectly civilised state" (4:34–35). Perhaps most tellingly, he always begins his discourses with that characteristic phrase of Enlightenment history: "In the infancy of society—" (4:70).

Like the Scottish Enlightenment historians too, Mr. Mac Quedy clearly looks to Scotland for his model of civilized society. To Reverend Folliot's generous (for Folliot) allowance in chapter 2 that the world could learn much from the Scots in "the art and science of fish for breakfast," Mac Quedy adds:

"And in many others, sir, I believe. Morals and metaphysics, politics and political economy, the way to make the most of all the modifications of smoke; steam, gas, and paper currency; you have all these to learn from us; in short, all the arts and sciences. We are the modern Athenians." (4:16)

But what are the contributions of the "modern Athenians" to civilized culture? When Reverend Folliot objects that "a sense of the beautiful" is essential to the true Athenian, Mac Quedy's philistine reply is "Then, sir, I presume you set no value on the right principles of rent, profit, wages, and currency" (4:16–17). Mr. Mac Quedy, indeed, goes so far as to claim that "the Athenians only sought the way, and we have found it; and to all this we have added political economy, the science of sciences" (4:21).

Mac Quedy's "science of sciences," like all other such intellectual panaceas in Peacock, is merely a idée fixe, although of a much more pernicious nature than landscaping or phrenology. To Mac Quedy, political economy is the highest achievement of his modern Athens, as indeed it is a legacy of the Scottish Enlightenment. This character embodies the eighteenth-century economic optimism of Adam Smith in an age dominated by the gloomy prognostications of David Ricardo. Where Smith had posited a natural identity of interests between men founded on the principle of sympathy, Ricardo, witnessing the class tensions of early nineteenth-century industrial society, based his doctrine on the assumption of a conflict of interests, depicting the modern commercial state as one in which all classes of society engaged in a vicious struggle for ascendancy. If Peacock, very much a child of the Enlightenment himself, could embrace Smith's economic optimism in the earlier *Genius of the Thames,* the intervening two decades had made such a sanguine outlook untenable, as his satire of "Scotch political economy" in the *Paper Money Lyrics* and *Crotchet Castle* testifies. Like other disaffected liberals of his time, Peacock was critical of some articles of Enlightenment faith, looking still to the Enlightenment for his ideal of civilized culture, while rejecting its optimistic progressivism.

It is against this background that we must view *Crotchet Castle.* The host-character of *Headlong Hall,* Squire Headlong, embodies the Enlightenment concept of "perfectibility." The antiquity of his Welsh lineage notwithstanding, he is an inveterate "improver," bent on cultivating both his understanding and the grounds of his estate. Although his "improving" projects often end catastrophically, he is nevertheless characterized by that indefatigable enthusiasm for innovation that to Enlightenment thinkers chiefly distinguished the human animal. Fittingly, it is he who, like the dukes and kings in Shakespearean comedy, presides over the multiple marriages that close the novel with their festive affirmation of civil society. By contrast, the host-character of *Crotchet Castle* represents a less creditable legacy of the Enlightenment. Mr. Crotchet is the progeny of

The Wealth of Nations, or, more accurately, of its debasement by the
"hyperbarbarous technology" (4:21) of the political economists. With
his fortune gained in the "alley" and his penchant for political
economy, Mr. Crotchet represents a cultural and social philistinism.
He is "half-informed," possessing only "a smattering of many things,
and a knowledge of none" (4:12). Proceeding in all his moral and
social views from the tenets of the "dismal science," this character
abjures charity "because he holds that all misfortune is from impru-
dence, that none but the rich ought to marry, and that all ought
to thrive by honest industry, as he did" (4:56). Dickens's Mr.
Bounderby is not far behind.

The bond of social union.   If a satisfactory resolution is reached
on the personal level in *Crotchet Castle,* such a resolution is only
partially glimpsed in the broader social context that frames the
story's love interest. Central to the novel in this respect is a debate
in chapters 9 and 10 between Mr. Mac Quedy and Mr. Chainmail
regarding the relative merits of past and present. Ostensibly the
dispute concerns itself with the historical accuracy of Sir Walter
Scott, whether he has misrepresented the Middle Ages, and if so,
whether by overidealizing them or depicting them as much worse
than they were. Mr. Mac Quedy dismisses them as "a period of
brutality, ignorance, fanaticism, and tyranny" (4:118). Mr. Chainmail, however, wonders whether the "religious spirit" of the Middle
Ages was not more socially beneficial than the "commercial spirit"
of the present age. "I do not see any compensation for that kindly
feeling which, within their own little communities, bound the
several classes of society together," he complains, for today "we have
no bond of union, but pecuniary interest" (4:123–24).

Thus this debate is concerned with more than the novels of Sir
Walter Scott. As Reverend Folliot says, "Gentlemen, you will never
settle this controversy, till you have first settled what is good for
man in this world" (4:121). The essence of the controversy is philosophical, then, involving much the same issues as the debate on
progress in *Headlong Hall.* In contrast to the earlier work's loftily
speculative dialogues on man and society, however, the debate in
Crotchet Castle is much more current, both in terms of its disputants
and its specific issues. Nevertheless, as in *Headlong Hall,* it is doubtful whether Peacock believes any clear-cut resolution to this debate
is possible, although something of a compromise will have been
suggested by the novel's end. In the meantime the question of "what

is good for man in this world" does not go unanswered in *Crotchet Castle*, even if the plethora of answers put forward threatens often to overwhelm the possibility of a single solution.

The first major debate on this question occurs in chapter 6. The scene is Crotchet Castle, and the debate is sponsored, ironically, by Crotchet, Jr., who announces that, money being all that is needed to regenerate society, he will provide a large sum for the purpose if the present company can agree on a way to dispose of it. Their goal is "a grand and universally applicable scheme for the amelioration of the condition of man" (4:81). The proposals are diverse and of varying degrees of usefulness:

MR. MAC QUEDY.
Build lecture rooms and schools for all.
MR. TRILLO.
Revive the Athenian theatre: regenerate the lyrical drama.
MR. TOOGOOD
Build a grand co-operative parallelogram, with a steam-engine in the middle for a maid of all work.
MR. FIREDAMP.
Drain the country, and get rid of *malaria,* by abolishing duck-ponds.
MR. MOROBIFIC.
Found a philanthropic college of anti-contagionists, where all the members shall be inoculated with the virus of all known diseases. Try the experiment on a grand scale.
MR. CHAINMAIL.
Build a great dining-hall: endow it with beef and ale, and hang the hall round with arms to defend the provisions.

(4:77–78)

Any chance of harmony among the above disputants appears unlikely, and Reverend Folliot advises Crotchet, Jr. to keep his money. The chapter ends, as such chapters often do in Peacock, with a drinking song, and "the schemes for the world's regeneration evaporated in a tumult of voices" (4:85).

Looking more closely, however, we find that Peacock has set up some interesting oppositions in this debate and, further, has obliquely suggested grounds for their reconciliation. Mac Quedy's is the dominant voice in the controversy, as his views reflect the economic orthodoxy that rules the world of *Crotchet Castle*. He proposes that "political economy is to the state what domestic economy is to the family" (4:73) and elicits some interesting responses. Folliot argues that the analogy is false because "in the family there is a *paterfamilias*" who ensures through a just distribution that there will be nothing of the gross inequality of the state, where there is "all hunger at one end, and all surfeit at the other" (4:73). The family, then, is a refuge for "kindly feeling" amidst the general heartlessness of a commercial society. Mr. Toogood the cooperationalist agrees that Folliot is onto something: "The reverend gentleman has hit the nail on the head. It is the distribution that must be looked to: it is the *paterfamilias* that is wanting in the state" (4:75).

Robert Owen, on whom Mr. Toogood is based, deplored the "jarring interests" arising from commercialism, which he felt were "on the extreme point of severing all the old connexions of society."[6] His factory at New Lanark was an attempt to adapt the paternalist rural tradition of feudalism to urban industrial society. Founded on the concept of a reciprocity of obligation between men rather than on economic interest, it thus violated the free-market tenets of political economy. In *Crotchet Castle* Mr. Toogood similarly refutes the doctrines of Mr. Mac Quedy. Moreover, a partial alliance is effected between Mr. Toogood and Reverend Folliot, as against the "dismal science," in their concurrence on the need for a regulatory and benevolent *"paterfamilias."* The difference, of course, lies in the fact that Folliot speaks only of the individual family, while Toogood speaks collectively—his *"paterfamilias"* comprehends society as a whole and refers specifically to the communal system of New Lanark. To this peculiar alliance we must also add Mr. Chainmail, for what is the "great dining hall" he envisages but the feudal version of Mr. Toogood's *"paterfamilias"?* Later, when Mr. Chainmail reiterates the need for a stronger "bond of union" in society than mere "pecuniary interest," he is seconded by Folliot, who states:

"I say, the nation is best off, in relation to other nations, which has the greatest quantity of the common necessaries of life distributed among the greatest number of persons; which has the greatest number of honest hearts and stout arms united in a common interest, willing to offend no one, but ready to fight in defence of their own community against all the rest of the world, because they have something in it worth fighting for." (4:127).

Thus perhaps the "tumult of voices" that ends such debates has a semblance of harmony after all. Certainly there are signs here of a consistent, if diversely constituted, alternative to Mac Quedy's "pound-shilling-and-pence philosophy," one, moreover, which promotes social over economic interest.

A viable alternative, however, emerges only at the novel's end. The genuine "bond of union," so lacking in the modern commercial state, is realized momentarily amidst the baronial splendor of Chainmail Hall in chapter 18. The occasion is Christmas, and the guests include, besides the Crotchet Castle regulars, Mr. Chainmail's neighbors and his tenants and domestics. All of them, "gentle and simple," sit together in the same room at long wooden tables, the line of social demarcation being simply an open fireplace in the center of the hall (4:193–94). The dominant idea here is social union, and the model is medieval communalism. But Peacock is not so backward-looking as to abandon the present entirely. Mr. Chainmail's "community of kind feelings" (4:204) owes a debt equally to Mr. Toogood's more modern brand of communalism. In his *Report to the County of New Lanark* (1821), for example, Owen envisages factory communities where "the food of the inhabitants may be prepared in one establishment, where they will eat together as one family"[7]—in effect, the old baronial halls of Scott's medieval novels, but on a larger scale and adapted to the changed needs of the age.

Indeed, that the solution lies in a kind of synthesis of feudal solidarity and enlightened reform is demonstrated by the mêlée that briefly interrupts these revels. At the height of the celebrations a mob of rioters announces itself outside with "a chorus of discordant voices" (4:199). We are abruptly brought back to the present with its sometimes violent social unrest, and indeed informing the incident is the fear of working-class revolution that haunted nineteenth-century England. However, rather than discrediting the ideas of Mr. Chainmail, this jarring intrusion actually serves to support them, as it is the combined force of the diverse company assembled here that saves the day. Momentarily forgetting their differences to defend Chainmail Hall, Mac Quedy, Folliot, Trillo, and the rest constitute what Folliot has earlier called for—"honest hearts and stout arms with a common interest." As Mr. Chainmail insists, following the successful rout of the mob, "The twelfth century has backed you well. Its manners and habits, its community of kind feelings between master and man, are the true remedy for these ebullitions" (4:204). Our own reservation in this regard is that Mr. Chainmail's "community of kind feelings" simply does not extend far enough. What of everyone outside Chainmail Hall? What of the rioters? This is surely what Mr. Toogood means when he gives to Mr. Chainmail's panegyric of the twelfth century his, significantly qualified, assent: "Something like it: improved by my diagram: arts for arms" (4:204).

The values that are brought out in this concluding episode, then, have finally nothing to do with medieval armor or wassail bowls or any of the other accoutrements of Chainmail Hall, but with social union—albeit on a limited scale, for such ideal societies in Peacock's novels are precarious things, kept secure by their isolation from the world outside—with ties stronger than those of mere "pecuniary interest." And here, despite the absurd excesses of their respective crotchets, is where Mr. Chainmail the feudalist and Mr. Toogood the cooperationalist concur, and the other guests of Chainmail Hall with them. It is this spirit that closes the novel—in the dance "in which all classes of the company mingled," even in the "mellifluous concert of noses," which follows as the fatigued guests eventually retire from the celebrations (4:206, 211).

Gryll Grange (1861)

When Peacock published his last novel, *Gryll Grange,* in 1861, he was seventy-six years of age, and thirty years had elapsed since his previous novel. Duties at the East India Company offer at least a partial explanation for his three-decade silence as a novelist: his key role in the company's adoption of steam navigation, not to mention his subsequent supervision of the construction of the first steamships, must have occupied his main energies. In 1836 he assumed the direction of the Examiner's Office in the company, succeeding James Mill in that position. His personal life too had not been free from distraction. With his mother's death in 1833— after which, as he told a friend, "he wrote with no interest"—he was left to care for an invalid wife and three children. After his retirement from the India House in 1856, now a widower, he lost both his daughters, Rosa Jane in 1857, and Mary Ellen Meredith, following a marriage scandal, in 1861.

Nevertheless, *Gryll Grange* (1861) shows little apparent evidence of the thirty-year gap separating it from the other novels. But for certain of its topical concerns, it might have been written shortly after *Crotchet Castle.* The basic format of the novel of talk remains

intact: an idyllic country-house setting, a genial host, several opinionated guests, and a romantic love interest. Its sole concession to
the age of Dickens seems to have been serial publication in *Fraser's
Magazine* in 1860 (it appeared in book form the following year). In
fictional terms, however, the great Victorian novelists might not
have written, for their imprint is nowhere evident in *Gryll Grange*.
In this his last novel, "The Author of *Headlong Hall*," as he is called
on the title page, retains his characteristic fictional form.

Perhaps it was this very quality of anachronism that gave *Gryll
Grange* its novelty when it first appeared. The *Saturday Review* was
struck chiefly, it seems, by its quaint charm:

The volume reads like a few numbers of *Notes and Queries* jumbled up with
a funny love story, and pervaded by a fine Pagan morality. The greatest
tribute to its merits that can be paid is to say—what may be said with
perfect truth—that all this queer mixture flows easily along, and that we
never feel that we have been delivered over to a learned bore. (1:cci–ccii)

Other reviews were similarly favorable. Indeed, the poet Tennyson
is said to have admired the novel (1:cci).

Gryll Grange has been with some justice called "an old man's
book,"[8] but there is nothing in its satire to suggest that Peacock
found the decades following the first Reform Bill less interesting
than those preceding it. The preface to a new edition of *Melincourt*
published in 1856 is anything but valedictory:

Of the disputants whose opinions and public characters (for I never tres-
passed on private life) were shadowed in some of the persons of the story,
almost all have passed from the diurnal scene. Many of the questions,
discussed in the dialogues, have more of general than of temporary application, and have still their advocates on both sides: and new questions
have arisen, which furnish abundant argument for similar conversations,
and of which I may yet, perhaps, avail myself on some future occasion.
(2:2–3).

The allusion to *Gryll Grange,* or something like it, is unmistakable.
If this work was unaffected by the revolution that the English novel
underwent in the age of Dickens, it could not be said to have been
unaffected by the issues of that age. "Similar conversations" fur-
nished with argument from "new questions" is an apt description
of Peacock's last novel.

The enchanted garden. If he is not one of Peacock's more memorable hosts, Mr. Gryll is nevertheless one of the more contented:

Gregory Gryll, Esq., of Gryll Grange in Hampshire, on the borders of the New Forest, in the midst of a park which was a little forest in itself, reaching nearly to the sea, and well stocked with deer, having a large outer tract, where a numerous light-rented and well-conditioned tenantry fattened innumerable pigs, considered himself well located for what he professed to be, *Epicuri de grege porcus.* (5:13)

As well as being "a pig from the herd of Epicurus," Mr. Gryll believes himself to be lineally descended from Gryllus: in Homer's *Odyssey* a shipwrecked Greek who, transformed into a hog, chose to remain a beast in the enchanted garden of Circe despite the exhortations of Odysseus. Although here, as elsewhere in Peacock, Epicureanism frequently shows itself in copious amounts of song and drink, its more temperate, philosophical aspect is also evident. If Mr. Gryll likes to dine well, he also likes to dine quietly, at a table where civilized, informed talk is the rule. The chief value at Gryll Grange, then, is the epicurean one of mental tranquillity, and Mr. Gryll's household, in Peacock's opening accounts, is characterized by an atmosphere of "quiet enjoyment" (5:16).

Indeed, unusual for a host in Peacock, Mr. Gryll seems to allow at his table only "questions which might afford ample room for pleasant conversation and none for acrimonious dispute" (5:15). Thus it is not surprising that the eccentric disputants who provide much of the fare in the other novels of talk are virtually absent here. The only bona fide crotcheteers in *Gryll Grange* are Mr. Minum the composer and Mr. Pallet the painter; beyond one very temperate debate in chapter 14 on the use of counterpoint and perspective in ancient Greek music and painting respectively, they are largely silent. Mr. MacBorrowdale is a political economist and, what is more, a Scotsman, but he is a congenial figure, not in the least given to the windy dogmatism of *Crotchet Castle*'s Mr. Mac Quedy. Similarly, Mr. Gryll's friend, Reverend Doctor Opimian, resembles Reverend Folliot only in his fondness for classical learning and good wine. Like the gods of Epicurus, he lives "above the cares of the world" that so exercise Folliot (5:18–19).

The epicurean gods were immortal, however, and the characters of *Gryll Grange* are not. Mr. Gryll believes that "the actual state of things admitted no change for the better" (5:16), but of course change must come. Although he traces his ancestry to the palace of Circe, Mr. Gryll has taken little care for his posterity. His one hope for descendants is an orphan niece named Morgana, but "her departure from his house would be the severest blow that fate could inflict on him" (5:16). Similarly, another character, the eccentric, tower-dwelling Algernon Falconer, has "aimed at living, like an ancient Epicurean, a life of tranquillity" (5:102–3). Served by seven chaste maidens and enjoying exclusively intellectual pursuits, he seeks to avoid any possibility of change, for his reclusive existence is predicated on a fear of the future. Even in the midst of the natural beauty that surrounds his tower refuge, he is inconsolable. "Very beautiful for the actual present—too beautiful for the probable future," he laments, since someday the forest will disappear. "The more we admire it now, the more we shall regret it then" (5:33).

It is this state of affairs on which *Gryll Grange* opens, but change is imminent. "It is vain to make schemes of life," warns Reverend Opimian. "The world will have its slaves, and so will Love" (5:103). The novel's main plot revolves around the tentative courtship of Falconer and Morgana, complicated by the presence of a second suitor for Miss Gryll's hand, the faddish Lord Curryfin. The latter is eventually paired off with a second female character, Miss Niphet, but not before Mr. Falconer is rudely shaken out of his unworldly schemes of life. Peacock's comment on this final development—resulting in no less than nine marriages, including those of the seven sisters who formerly served Falconer—is sympathetic but firm: "It was the dissipation of a dream too much above mortal frailty, too much above the contingencies of chance and change, to be permanently realized" (5:374).

A victory for love, moreover, is also a victory for the world in this novel. The device by which Peacock draws his characters together is the Aristophanic comedy, staged in chapter 28, in which all participate. As well as developing *Gryll Grange*'s various love interests, this play within the novel provides a window on the age. Entitled "Aristophanes in London," it exposes modern folly and draws into a focus the various cultural and social concerns that run through *Gryll Grange*. As Falconer tells Reverend Opimian, even the epicurean Garden of Pleasure is not proof against outside concerns:

"It is not my own world I complain of. It is the world on which I look
'from the loop-holes of retreat.' I cannot sit here, like one of the Gods of
Epicurus, who, as Cicero says, was satisfied with thinking, through all
eternity, 'how comfortable he was.' I look with feelings of intense pain
on the mass of poverty and crime; of unhealthy, unavailing, unremunerated
toil, blighting childhood in its blossom, and womanhood in its prime; of
'all the oppressions that are done under the sun.' " (5:92)

The rhetoric of this passage indicates that Peacock was still thinking
of Shelley in 1860 (the third and final part of his "Memoirs" of
Shelley was published in *Fraser's Magazine* during this year, as was
Gryll Grange), and the character of Falconer himself may be partially
based on Peacock's memories of his old friend, as commentators
have claimed. In any case, there is much in *Gryll Grange* to suggest
that the author of *Melincourt,* now in his old age, was not only still
troubled by what he saw around him, but was still actively engaged
with such issues as a writer.

    A poetic faith.   According to John Stuart Mill, "religion and
poetry address themselves . . . to the same part of the human
constitution: they both supply the same want, that of conceptions
grander and more beautiful than we see realized in the prose of
human life."[9] Religion and poetry play an important role in *Gryll
Grange,* both representing what is lacking in the world of the present. When in chapter 1 Reverend Opimian suggests the possibility
of holding a poetic disputation in the manner of the twelfth-century
tenson, Miss Gryll rejects the idea, saying, "I am afraid, Doctor,
our age is too prosy for that sort of thing" (5:9). This is a familiar
strain in Peacock, and yet it seems particularly insistent in *Gryll
Grange.*

    As the *Saturday Review* remarked, *Gryll Grange* is "pervaded by
a fine Pagan morality," and Algernon Falconer, who has piously
modeled his household after certain aspects of Homeric domestic
life, is certainly a worthy votary of the old religion. But *Gryll Grange*
is far from being a relic of Peacock's Hellenism. Falconer's chosen
mode of life reflects other religious preoccupations as well. If the
seven sisters who serve him—his "household deities" (5:209)—
provide dinner entertainment in the manner of Homer's Greece,
they also close every evening with a hymn to St. Catherine. Falconer's
own bedchamber, moreover, is a virtual shrine to this saint, dis-
playing an altar with her image and panels painted with subjects

from her life (5:72). Peacock himself appears to have carried on a kind of devotion to St. Catherine, which a few of his acquaintances mistook for a leaning toward Catholicism. [10] In Falconer's case, there is a question of this too, although he takes pains to assure Reverend Opimian that Catherine is a saint of the Reformed Church, and the latter seems satisfied that his young friend, if not quite orthodox, is safely within the pale of the Church of England (5:65).

Falconer's curious religious preoccupations may also have reference to the controversy surrounding the Oxford Movement (also known as the Tractarian Movement). Initiated at Oxford in the 1830s, this movement was headed by John Henry Newman and was aimed primarily at combating the scientific skepticism that was undermining faith, and at restoring some of the dignity and zeal of the early English Church. Some, however, were alarmed by the adoption of certain doctrines and forms of worship that they regarded as purely Roman Catholic, and a controversy ensued. Although most intense during the 1840s, the controversy continued into the decades following and was characterized by bitter polemics, most notably in the famous exchange between Newman and Charles Kingsley. In this context, Falconer's Catholic sympathies are especially significant. Even such, relatively speaking, cursory allusions to Anglo-Catholicism as appear in *Gryll Grange* would surely have been noted by contemporary readers after the polemics of the previous two decades.

Gryll Grange avoids the factiousness of the period's Tractarian and anti-Tractarian literature. There are perhaps traces of sectarian bias in Reverend Opimian's concerned speculation about Falconer's dubious orthodoxy and in certain of the exchanges between the two men. There is no sustained religious controversy in *Gryll Grange,* however, and Peacock himself does not take sides, beyond betraying some temperamental propensity for the Catholic ambience. As with such various subjects as political economy and landscape gardening in previous novels, Peacock is interested in the Tractarian controversy for its broader cultural implications. Falconer's religious enthusiasms are a reaction to the excessive rationalism and vulgarity of modern life, and a craving for something higher, more ideal. "I feel the necessity of some such devotion, to fill up the void which the world, as it is, leaves in my mind," he tells Reverend Opimian (5:78). Is, then, Falconer's preoccupation religious or aesthetic? A character in the novel named Dr. Anodyne takes the latter view, that it arises "less from faith than from a certain feeling of poetry" (5:93–94). Reverend Opimian, however, is inclined to regard it as containing elements of both, describing this devotion as "one of the many forms of the love of ideal beauty, which, without being in itself religion, exerts on vivid imaginations an influence that is very often like it" (5:94).

It is this disposition of mind—variously described as "a form of aestheticism" (5:32) and a "sort of spiritualism" (5:55)—that is responsible for the air of quasi-religion that pervades *Gryll Grange.* The "enchanted garden," whether that of Epicurus or Circe, is a frequent image, and magic is often invoked, if not as an actual fact, at least as a possibility. Morgana Gryll, for example, named for an enchantress in Ariosto's epic *Orlando Furioso,* is a believer in magic of sorts. Comparing the poets Berni and Bojardo in chapter 20, she favors Bojardo because he "seems to have more faith in his narrative than Berni. I go on with him with ready credulity, where Berni's pleasantry interposes a doubt" (5:206). Just as Mr. Falconer is eventually caught under Morgana's spell, so Lord Curryfin, for all his scientific enthusiasms, is captivated by the mystery surrounding the enigmatic Miss Niphet. In the Aristophanic comedy even spirit-rapping can be supposed to be "dramatically" true (5:10), while in chapter 34 ("Christmas Tales") every manner of ghost story is accorded a "ready faith" (5:358). Just as Miss Gryll rejects, in the latter connection, supernatural tales that include rational explanations, Mr. Falconer favors saints' legends, thus endorsing poetic, as against scientific, truth.

Curiously, Peacock's tolerance in matters supernatural does not extend to the popular vogue of Spiritualism, then at its height. If spirit-rapping can be supposed, by a valid act of poetic faith, to be dramatically true, in itself it is a "monstrous" instance of "human credulity," according to Reverend Opimian: "It is thought something wonderful that uneducated persons should believe in witchcraft in the nineteenth century: as if educated persons did not believe in grosser follies: such as this same spirit-rapping, unknown tongues, clairvoyance, table-turning, and all sorts of fanatical impositions" (5:11).

The central conceit of the Aristophanic comedy presented in chapter 28 is its curious association of Spiritualism and material progress. Mythical and historical figures from the past are summoned up by the London Spirit-rapping Society, who attempt to impress them with the "scientific wonders" of the nineteenth century (5:281). In contrast to the poetic faith of Falconer and Morgana, there is something singularly worldly about the machinery of Spiritualism. Contemporary critics ridiculed spiritualists for their bogus air of scientific validity, and, not surprisingly, charges of fraud were common.[11] One of the "grosser follies" of the age, in Reverend Opimian's view, Spiritualism is finally only a mechanical trick, like the rational explanations to ghost stories which Morgana deplores as mere "sleights of hand" (5:358). As a climax to the Aristophanic comedy, the table of the spirit-rappers begins to spin around with ever-accelerating speed, and then dances off the stage, followed by the spirit-rappers who are pursued by their chairs—an impressive "piece of mechanical pantomime" and a "triumph of Lord Curryfin's art" (5:290), but a contrived effect nevertheless, a sleight of hand as much attesting to the fallacy of trusting solely in material progress as to the trickery of fraudulent spiritualists. As Mr. MacBorrowdale observes of the age:

"Tables turn as usual, and the ghost-trade appears to be thriving: for instead of being merely audible, the ghosts are becoming tangible, and shake hands under the tables with living wiseacres, who solemnly attest the fact. Civilized men ill-use their wives; the wives revenge themselves in their own way, and the Divorce Court has business enough on its hands to employ it twenty years at its present rate of progression. Commercial bubbles burst, and high-pressure boilers blow up, and mountebanks of all descriptions flourish on public credulity". (5:319).

Indeed, a blind and uncritical faith in progress is perhaps the most dangerous superstition of all.

Science and wisdom. According to Peacock in his 1857 preface to *Melincourt,* unreflecting quantification characterizes the age in all matters:

The progress of intellect, with all deference to those who believe in it, is not quite so obvious as the progress of mechanics. The "reading public" has increased its capacity of swallow, in a proportion far exceeding that of its digestion. Thirty-nine years ago, steamboats were just coming into action, and the railway locomotive was not even thought of. Now everybody goes everywhere: going for the sake of going, and rejoicing in the rapidity with which they accomplish nothing. *On va, mais on ne voyage pas.* Strenuous idleness drives us on the wings of steam in boats and trains, seeking the art of enjoying life, which, after all, is in the regulation of the mind, and not in the whisking about of the body. (2:2).

To all appearances, the characters of *Gryll Grange* have escaped this aspect of their age. Indeed, Morgana Gryll seems to have rejected a past suitor on this very count, one Mr. Enavant. "I had no fancy for living in an express train," she explains. "I like to go quietly through life, and to see all that lies in my way" (5:371). Miss Gryll expresses the preference of a number of Victorians, Matthew Arnold and John Ruskin among them, for a more reflective and humane perspective, and of course she is criticizing a pervasive aspect of modern culture. In the world depicted in *Gryll Grange* high-pressure steam locomotion is on a par with competitive examinations, fashionable lectures, and popular education. "The test of intellectual capacity is in swallow, and not in digestion" (5:2), complains one character, just as "going, for the sake of going" (5:281) seems the sole rationale for the accelerated rate of modern life.

The diffusion of knowledge is the province of Pantopragmatics in *Gryll Grange.* Under the presidency of Lord Facing-both-ways (based on Henry Brougham, a proponent of popular education and anathema to Peacock), the Pantopragmatic Society has dedicated itself to nothing less than the diffusion of every species of knowledge through every class of society. Far from representing any kind of fruitful synthesis, however, Pantopragmatics is only another source of undigested and useless information. "Like most other science," observes Reverend Opimian, "it resolves itself into lecturing, lecturing, lecturing, about all sorts of matters, relevant and irrelevant" (5:68). Thus it complements perfectly the competitive-examination mentality with its undiscriminating regard for mere acquisition rather than understanding. A passage from Newman's *The Idea of a University* (1852) describes the attitude of mind embodied generally by Pantopragmatics and specifically by one Lord Curryfin, a lecturing nobleman and associate of the Pantopragmatic Society:

I will tell you, Gentlemen, what has been the practical error of the last twenty years—not to load the memory of the student with a mass of undigested knowledge, but to force upon him so much that he has rejected all. It has been the error of distracting and enfeebling the mind by an unmeaning profusion of subjects; and of implying that a smattering in a dozen branches of study is not shallowness, which it really is, but enlargement, which it is not; of considering an acquaintance with the learned names of things and persons, and the possession of clever duodecimos, and attendance on eloquent lectures, and membership with scientific institutions, and the sight of the experiments of a platform and the specimens of a museum, that all this was not dissipation of mind, but progress.[12]

Lord Curryfin belongs to the class of amiable enthusiasts in Peacock, such as *Nightmare Abbey*'s Mr. Asterias, also a scientist. Personally, he is a very appealing figure, energetic and possessed of unceasing energy. But although his abilities are impressive, there is something in his use of them that suggests the "shallowness" noted by Newman in the age. He has "a strong memory, much power of application, and a facility of learning rapidly" (5:113– 14), and yet he seems incapable of sticking to anything: "He was readily taken by novelty in doctrine, and followed a new lead with great pertinacity" (5:114). With all his "multifarious attainments" Lord Curryfin represents the intellectual dissipation that Newman believed had enfeebled the modern mind by overwhelming it with "an unmeaning profusion of subjects"—unmeaning because there is no real philosophy behind it, and hence no real understanding. "A smattering of a hundred things or a memory for detail is not a philosophical or comprehensive view," says Newman. "Recreations are not education; accomplishments are not education."[13]

Initially both rivals for the hand of Morgana Gryll, Lord Curryfin and Mr. Falconer are cast as different aspects of the modern temper: Curryfin as unreflecting science and Falconer as excessively introspective humanism. This is not to schematize them as personified cultural vices in a kind of nineteenth-century morality play, but only to suggest what is intended in part by Peacock's depiction of them as rival suitors. The choice of a suitor, and with it the choice of a philosophy, is always an important matter in Peacock. In Lord Curryfin and Mr. Falconer we have two very different suitors and philosophies.

Lord Curryfin has the resolution, indeed the often necessary impulsiveness, to carry through his designs, whether they concern untested inventions or marriage. He not only welcomes innovation, but falls in with it too rashly perhaps, as with Pantopragmatics or his sometimes ill-fated experiments. In the latter connection, we frequently view him in perilous situations—if not trying out an untested (and flawed) design for a sailboat (chapter 16), then breaking an untamed horse or experimenting with a newly invented "high phaeton" (chapter 17). In one way or another, then, he is identified with the impulsiveness of the age, in the spheres of both intellect and action. In his lectures and conversation he skims carelessly over a miscellany of subjects that, however briefly, have caught his fancy, while in rash experiments he courts disaster as surely as high-pressure steam is symptomatic of the age's destructive mania for speed. What he never does, however, is take time to reflect—and this Mr. Falconer does do, to the extent that he does very little else.

Where his rival thoughtlessly exposes himself to dangers of every kind, Mr. Falconer does not take enough risks. His courtship of Morgana Gryll nearly fails through his indecision, convinced as he is that "marriage is at best a dangerous experiment" (5:107). If Lord Curryfin is always depicted in action, Mr. Falconer is always shown in contemplation. In chapter 24, for example, when the former ice-skates with Miss Niphet, "Mr. Falconer was there, and contented himself with looking on" (5:246). Similarly, in the preceding chapter, while Lord Curryfin and Miss Niphet are again featured center-stage, this time dancing, Falconer "continued to sit," reflecting on his diminishing prospects with Morgana—and yet "he dared not try the experiment" (5:244).

Clearly what is needed is balance, for each character possesses those very qualities lacked by the other. Lord Curryfin acts, but fails to reflect, and the reverse is true of Falconer. A realization of this strikes Falconer at one point in chapter 20, as he pines for Morgana, and if he fails to act until nearer the novel's end, his resolution here at least points toward a proper balance of thought and action. "Whatever I may do should be done calmly, deliberately, philosophically," he decides, "than suddenly, passionately, impulsively"—a dictum which Lord Curryfin would do well to observe—but Falconer also realizes that "it is now or never: this or none" (5:212). Eventually, he is compelled to act, just as Lord Curryfin is more or less compelled to reflect, on his feelings for Miss Niphet, and, more important, on her feelings for him. In the latter connection, indeed, Lord Curryfin suffers unwonted perplexity and is successful in his suit only after he agrees to a ban on further dangerous experiments. Thereafter, Miss Niphet is his "guiding star" (5:374). "Love, adoration, absorption of all feelings into one" (5:314) replace "multifarious" and "protean" pursuits as this grave and reflective young woman becomes the focus for Lord Curryfin's wayward intellect. "We ought to have more wisdom," comments Reverend Opimian during a discussion of modern culture, "as we have clearly more science" (5:186), and this is the underlying message of *Gryll Grange*.

Chapter Six
Maid Marian and
The Misfortunes of Elphin:
Satiric Romance

Appearing in the decade following the publication of Peacock's first three novels of talk, the satiric romances—*Maid Marian* (1822) and *The Misfortunes of Elphin* (1829)—represent something of a new direction for Peacock. As specimens of historical romance they have affinities with the poetry, particularly the Ossianic imitations, for they are products of a nostalgia for the past that characterizes much romantic literature. They depart from the poetry, however, in retaining the comic-satiric elements found in the novels of talk. In this respect the satiric romances are in the line of Peacock's most characteristic work. They differ from his other fiction chiefly in their greater emphasis on narrrative as opposed to dialogue, and in their historical settings. In the novels of talk, with their modern settings, the past is continually evoked through allusion, while the inverse is true of the romances. If their action is set exclusively in the past, their themes have a more recent stamp, and the reader is invited to take stock of modern society through comparison.

Maid Marian (1822)

An entry in Peacock's diary for August 1818 first mentions *Maid Marian:* "Could not read or write for scheming my romance. Rivers castles forests abbies monks maids kings and banditti dancing before me like a masked ball" (8:440). Indeed, this is an apt description of the finished work, for *Maid Marian* suggests nothing so much as a "masked ball," its characters and setting seeming to be just so many stage properties. Considering the vogue that surrounded the medieval novels of Sir Walter Scott, perhaps it is not surprising that Peacock should have tried his hand at one himself: a prefatory note to *Maid Marian* indicates that he worried about close parallels being drawn being this work and *Ivanhoe,* which had appeared in 1820. Such a fear was groundless, however. No trace of Scott's historical realism can be detected among the troupe of "monks maids kings and banditti" who dance across the stage in *Maid Marian.* If anything, this work has more in common with the romantic comedies of Shakespeare, such as *As You Like It* and *Much Ado About Nothing,* with their idyllic settings and witty characters.

Although it was begun and mainly composed in the latter part of 1818, *Maid Marian* was not published until 1822, when Peacock wrote the last three chapters. The delay was undoubtedly due to new duties at the India House, taken up in 1819, and Peacock left unfinished some other works at the same time, including his "Essay on Fashionable Literature." When the novel did appear, a friend wrote to Mary Shelley: "Peacock's *Maid Marian* I think a beautiful little thing, but it has not taken yet" (1:cx). Apart from a brief piece in the *Monthly Magazine* commending its "quaint humour" (1:cx), *Maid Marian* received scant notice until it appeared at Covent Garden in the form of an opera in late 1822. The actor Charles Kemble had apparently been taken by the novel—for even in its fictional form *Maid Marian* has obvious light operatic qualities— and arranged to have it adapted for the stage. The success of the stage version served to bring the novel to greater public attention. The *Literary Gazette* and the *Literary Chronicle* reviewed it favorably, if belatedly, while notices of the opera gave it complimentary mention as well.

While not Peacock's most characteristic work, *Maid Marian* has been a favorite with readers drawn by its pleasant mixture of pastoralism and wit. It does have topical concerns, however, and to this extent it exhibits unmistakable satiric intent. "I am writing a comic Romance of the Twelfth Century," Peacock wrote to Shelley in 1818, "which I shall make the vehicle of much oblique satire on all the oppressions that are done under the sun" (8:209). Peacock was being deliberately hyperbolic here, of course—perhaps he was recalling Shelley's early misconceptions about the satire of *Nightmare Abbey*—but in certain of its concerns *Maid Marian* bears discussion within the context of Peacock's satire.

Barons and bandits. In its opening, at least, *Maid Marian* appears to offer Peacock's typical setting of the idyllic rural retreat. Rather than a country house, however, this is a twelfth-century abbey:

The abbey of Rubygill stood in a picturesque valley, at a little distance from the western boundary of Sherwood Forest, in a spot which seemed adapted by nature to be the retreat of monastic mortification, being on the banks of a fine trout-stream, and in the midst of woodland coverts, abounding with excellent game. (3:1)

Gathered here in chapter 1 are the wedding party of Robert Fitz-Ooth, Earl of Locksley and Huntington, and Matilda Fitzwater, daughter of the Baron of Arlingford. But before the nuptials can be completed, a troop of the king's men intrudes to seize Robert Fitz-Ooth on a charge of treason. It seems that the latter has violated the "forest laws" by poaching the king's deer, and in addition is deeply in debt to a wealthy abbot. Thus an enemy to church and state, he has been declared an outlaw. A battle ensues, during which Fitz-Ooth and his men fight their way out and find sanctuary in Sherwood Forest, where they become known as Robin Hood and his band of merry men.

Matilda, meanwhile, has been kept in confinement by her father. But, as the baron well knows, his daughter's mind "is as hard to change as nature and the elements" (3:30), and Matilda soon escapes to rejoin her lover in Sherwood Forest. Matilda, or Maid Marian as she is known among the outlaws, is one of Peacock's more memorable and attractive female characters. A skillful archer, she clearly favors the hunt over sedentary female occupations. She is a match for her father, the fiercely choleric baron, and does not hesitate to loose an arrow at a priest, or even duel with a king at one point. Peacock briefly sketches in chapter 4 the fine balance of passion and grace that characterizes her: "Her black eyes sparkled like sunbeams on a river: a clear, deep, liquid radiance, the reflection of ethereal fire,—tempered, not subdued, in the medium of its living and gentle mirror" (3:33).

Another character who takes refuge in Sherwood is the errant Friar Michael, who takes the name of Friar Tuck among his outlaw brethren. His vows notwithstanding, this "profane, roaring, bawl-ing, bumper-bibbing, neck-breaking, catch-singing friar" (3:40) is very much a Falstaffian character, possessing vital physical appetites and, unlike his Shakespearean prototype, dauntless courage. He anticipates in some respects Peacock's famous drunkard, Prince Seithenyn, of *The Misfortunes of Elphin,* with whom he shares a talent for political sophistry. It is Friar Tuck who expounds the theory of Robin's "forest republic."

The other characters of the tale, including Robin Hood himself, are less memorable, resembling stock dramatic types more than anything else. None of Peacock's eccentric crotcheteers appears in this work. The only caricature of a contemporary personality is Harpiton, Prince John's venal and obsequious court minstrel, who is loosely based on Robert Southey. As Poet Laureate, Southey was a figure of contempt to liberal writers like Shelley and Byron, who mocked his poetic effusions in honor of Europe's various crowned heads. Thus Harpiton is always ready "to undertake at a moment's notice any kind of courtly employment, called dirty work by the profane, which the blessings of civil government, namely, his master's pleasure, and the interests of social order, namely, his own emolument, might require" (3:88). Significantly, a pirated edition of *Wat Tyler,* a play written by Southey during his youthful radical phase in the 1790s, had been published the year before Peacock began *Maid Marian.* Like Peacock's work set in the Middle Ages, *Wat Tyler* is the story of an honest blacksmith who is forced to turn outlaw following an incident with the king's tax collectors. As in *Maid Marian* too, it sets natural equality, represented by Tyler and his outlaw followers, against the arbitrary prescriptive authority of the king's forces. Needless to say, the now politically orthodox Poet Laureate was embarrassed by this reminder of his radical youth, and in *Maid Marian* Peacock offers a nicely pointed allusion to the minor controversy occasioned by *Wat Tyler's* belated publication.

Maid Marian's plot develops along characteristically desultory lines. Prince John is apparently infatuated with Matilda, and for this reason has laid siege to her father's castle. He is not successful, but the old baron is forced to flee his lands and go into hiding with Robin and his men. The rest of the story is constructed mainly of traditional episodes from the Robin Hood legends—for example, Robin's famous duel with Friar Tuck on the river (chapter 16). During the course of the narrative, sundry prosperous citizens are relieved of their wealth for the charity of the poor, and several battles are fought. In the end, a strange knight who receives Robin's hospitality reveals himself to be King Richard, newly returned from the Crusades, and restores to Robin and his men their rightful titles and estates. However, when, following Richard's death, Prince John

takes the throne, the foresters find themselves compelled once more
to take up their "greenwood sovereignty," and they live happily
together in merry Sherwood.

The court of nature.   In an otherwise savage review of Thomas
Moore's *The Epicurean,* published in the *Westminster Review* of 1827,
Peacock at one point sanctions a bit of historical license taken by
Moore. "As a light touch of satire, glancing from the past to the
present, all this is very well," he says (9:6). This approbation is
qualified, of course, for in most cases Peacock was a stickler for
historical accuracy. Yet his earlier cited description of *Maid Marian*
as a "vehicle of much oblique satire on all the oppressions that are
done under the sun" suggests a use of history very similar to that
which he observes in Moore. The premise of *Maid Marian,* as Peacock
once remarked to Shelley, is that "there is nothing new under the
political sun" (8:201).

Peacock's principal source for *Maid Marian* was an anthology of
the Robin Hood legends and ballads collected by Joseph Ritson, an
antiquarian and a political radical notoriously sympathetic to the
ideals of the French Revolution. In view of the latter circumstance,
it is not surprising that Ritson should present a Robin Hood seeming
to possess political views like his own. Thus Ritson's final summing
up of the outlaw's life bears unmistakably the imprint of his revolutionary fervor: "Such was the end of Robin Hood: a man who,
in a barbarous age, and under a complicated tyranny, displayed a
spirit of freedom and independence which has endeared him to the
common people, whose cause he maintained, (for all opposition to
tyranny is the cause of the people)."[1] Such historical anachronisms
run through *Maid Marian* as well. Passing references to King Richard, for example, make him sound like a kind of medieval Duke of
Wellington, an "arch-crusader and anti-jacobin by excellence" (3:86).
References to Sherwood Forest's "swinish multitude" of wild boars
(3:100) are clearly meant to recall the famous phrase Edmund Burke
once scornfully applied to the general populace. Egalitarian sentiments are reflected also in *Maid Marian*'s comic exposure of Tyrants
and Priests, and most notably in the forest republic established by
Robin and his men, which has its basis in "distributive justice"
(3:62).

Rather than being an egalitarian or a revolutionary, Peacock's
Robin Hood is an outlaw with egalitarian and revolutionary asso-

ciations. The outlaw is a common figure in romantic literature, appearing often in Byron and Scott, for example, where, if not explicitly political in his significance, he stands in an antagonistic relation to social convention. In William Godwin's *Caleb Williams* (1794) and Wordsworth's *The Borderers* (1795–96) the political implications of outlawry are made clear, and certainly Peacock's Robin Hood has emerged from this general romantic preoccupation with the figure of the outlaw. Moreover, actual outlaws of a radical turn of thinking were much in the news at this time. Jacobin-Carbonarist bandits in Italy were idealized by urban Jacobins during the period, and far from being mere peasant marauders these real-life outlaws often espoused a distinctly pre-socialist, left-wing ideology. The brigand Gaetano Vardarelli, for example, who was killed in 1818, the year in which most of *Maid Marian* was written, was a classic Robin Hood type. As well as distributing a portion of his booty to the poor, he apparently operated a sort of parallel underground government in the Italian peasants' interests, setting up his own tribunals and fulfilling the offices of a magistrate. As an outlaw he was exceptional, according to Eric Hobsbawm, in "his systematic pursuit of a more general justice."[2] The "high court of nature" established by Robin and his men in *Maid Marian* bears an interesting resemblance to Vardarelli's outlaw government with its courts and statutes.

Specifically, the outlaws' "high court of Nature" (3:100) is meant to satirize the cult of legitimacy embodied by the so-called Holy Alliance, which had established itself in Europe following the defeat of Napoleon in 1815. Comprising Austria, Russia, Prussia, France, and Britain, this alliance based its claims to legitimacy on the rather mystical doctrine of divine right. (Hence Mr. Anyside Antijack's endorsement, in *Melincourt*, of "legitimacy, divine right, the Jesuits, the Pope, the Inquisition, and the Virgin Mary's petticoat" [2:415]. Although it had a limited impact, the Holy Alliance suggested to some an alliance of kings against the people. Thus at one point in *Maid Marian* Peacock describes the "social order" of the twelfth century as being dedicated to

the preservation of the privileges of the few who happened to have any, at the expense of the swinish multitude who happened to have none, except that of working and being shot at for the benefit of their betters, which is obviously not the meaning of social order in our more enlightened times: let us therefore be grateful to Providence, and sing *Te Deum laudamus* in chorus with the Holy Alliance. (3:84)

As one instance of "oblique satire on all the oppressions that are done under the sun," this would undoubtedly have pleased Shelley as much as similar passages in *Melincourt.*

Just as the "legitimate" society from which Robin Hood and his men have fled has laws and institutions, however, so too does the forest dominion that they set up in Sherwood Forest have its own constitution. Although many of the principles on which Robin Hood's reign is based are admirable, the fact remains that its claim to legitimacy is no less arbitrary than that of the tyrannical Prince John; but then, as Peacock slyly suggests, it is no more so either. "Robin Hood," according to Friar Tuck, "is king of the forest both by dignity of birth and by virtue of his standing army: to say nothing of the free choice of his people, which he has indeed, but I pass it by as an illegitimate basis of power" (3:100). Friar Tuck's dismissal of popular choice as a basis for legitimacy seems inconsistent with the egalitarian associations surrounding Robin Hood in other connections. This is a result partly, no doubt, of irony on the friar's part, but also of Peacock's habitually double-edged satire. His liberalism notwithstanding, Peacock was as distrustful of arbitrary popular force as he was of prescriptive authority, and destructive mobs figure significantly in *Melincourt* and *Crotchet Castle.* For this reason, no character in *Maid Marian,* whether tyrant or outlaw, is entirely free of the ironic glance of his creator. Hence the purposefully dubious "articles of Legitimacy" put forward in chapter 12, which have as their premise "the one golden rule of right, consecrated by the universal consent of mankind, and by the practice of all ages, individuals, and nations: namely, To keep what we have, and to catch what we can" (3:110–11).

Unlike the hero of *Melincourt,* Mr. Forester, Maid Marian's Robin Hood is no philosopher and is not given to outlining the principles under which he operates. Friar Tuck is the figure responsible for articulating the outlaws' philosophical and political positions, although his speeches serve largely to invert parodically the present social order—things as they are in "the high court of Nature." Thus the laws and principles of this forest dominion, set out in chapter 12, suggest less a serious political program than a fool's court.

Nevertheless, despite his outlaw status, Robin Hood differs from a king like Richard only in his lack of "legitimacy," a dubious distinction at best, as Friar Tuck has pointed out:

"I say not that Richard is a thief, but I say that Robin is a hero: and for honour, did ever yet man, miscalled thief, win greater honour than Robin? Do not all men grace him with some honourable epithet? The most gentle thief, the most courteous thief, the most bountiful thief, yea, and the most honest thief? Richard is courteous, bountiful, honest, and valiant: but so also is Robin: it is the false word that makes the unjust distinction. They are twin-spirits, and should be friends, but that fortune hath differently cast their lot." (3:173)

And of course if the thief is not so much different from the king, there is the implication too that the king has points of similarity with the thief.

But Peacock's irony in *Maid Marian* is directed primarily at the forces of reaction. Although Friar Tuck's speeches often seem to present Sherwood Forest as a kind of ancien régime in microcosm, Robin Hood's sylvan retreat ultimately serves as satiric norm in *Maid Marian.* Outlawed by society, Robin and his followers exist in close relationship with nature. Like the Forest of Arden in Shakespeare's *As You Like It,* Sherwood Forest exists as a kind of innocent counterpart to the artificial life of court and city. It is associated with spring and youth—as in the May Day celebrations depicted in chapters 5 and 6 (a feature of Southey's *Wat Tyler* too, incidentally)—and the forest republic set up by the outlaws here is based on natural principles of equality and justice:

So Robin and Marian dwelt and reigned in the forest, ranging the glades and the greenwoods from the matins of the lark to the vespers of the nightingale, and administering natural justice according to Robin's ideas of rectifying the inequalities of human condition: raising genial dews from the bags of the rich and idle, and returning them in fertilising showers on the poor and industrious: an operation which more enlightened statesmen have happily reversed, to the unspeakable benefit of the community at large. (3:160)

That the reversal of such an "operation" is unnatural is made clear earlier in a more specific connection by Brother Michael who, to Baron Fitzwater's peremptory demand that Matilda be forced to re-

nounce her outlawed lover, counters: "Will I undertake . . . to
make Trent run westward, or to make the flame burn downward,
or to make a tree grow with its head in the earth and its root in
the air?" (3:30) Any social order based on such arbitrary prerogatives
necessarily exists in opposition to nature.

Despite, then, the occasional satiric parallels drawn by Friar Tuck
between it and any other government—whether that of Prince John
in the twelfth century or of Prime Minister Liverpool in the nineteenth—the society established in Sherwood Forest is presented
along the lines of similar utopian societies found elsewhere in Peacock. Robin Hood's concept of "natural justice," as he himself points
out in chapter 13, is derived from "Roman Law" (3:126), which
identifies this forest community with the early Roman Republic,
whence Mr. Forester draws the inspiration for the ideal agrarian
community maintained on his estate in *Melincourt*. Robin and his
men are not, of course, agriculturalists, yet their "greenwood liberty" is meant to represent a similarly equitable and natural conception of the social contract. As in the novels of talk, however,
Robin's forest republic represents an ideal realized on a limited scale.
Just as social harmony is achieved only within the walls of Chainmail
Hall in *Crotchet Castle,* and in *Headlong Hall* the pessimistic Mr.
Escot concedes the possibility of a change for the better only within
the personal sphere of marriage, so this sylvan refuge is a tiny, and
very precarious, retreat from the barbarous world outside.

Misfortunes of Elphin (1829)

Separated by seven years, *Maid Marian* and *The Misfortunes of
Elphin* share common characteristics. Both depict a picturesque and
in many ways ideal past that serves as a foil to the prosaic present.
Both are cast in a continuous narrative form with none of the extended symposia that typify the novels of talk. Moreover, despite
their period settings, both works make oblique satiric glances at
the present, and their sly anachronisms are deliberate and pointed.
Unlike the earlier romance, however, *The Misfortunes of Elphin* is
more ambitiously conceived. If, like *Maid Marian,* it has been
constructed from scraps of legend and tradition gleaned from antiquarian sources, its story is stronger and more continuous (notwithstanding Peacock's later comment that the work was wholly
conceived as a frame for his songs).[3] Similarly, *Maid Marian's* rough

knockabout and burlesque is absent from *The Misfortunes of Elphin,* replaced by a narrative structure in which events are more closely related to the intellectual themes of the work.

Peacock also seems to have put a great deal more research into this work than he had in *Maid Marian.* While it is doubtful that it was treated by Welsh antiquarians as "a serious and valuable addition to Welsh history," as a friend claimed (1:cxxxvii), *The Misfortunes of Elphin* reflects Peacock's extensive reading in Welsh history and mythology. He is said to have learned the Welsh language, probably with the help of his Welsh-speaking wife, and the list of his sources, probable and known, is impressive.[4] Indeed, even the curiously anachronistic blend of Celtic history and modern politics that characterizes *The Misfortunes of Elphin* is traceable to Peacock's sources—William Owen Pughe, for example, in whose antiquarian writings radical polemics figure as prominently as they do in Ritson.

Although its sales were moderate—it was not reprinted in either the 1837 or 1856 editions of Peacock's novels—*The Misfortunes of Elphin* did enjoy a favorable critical reception. The *Monthly Magazine* and *Literary Gazette* were unqualified in their praise. The *Westminster Review,* though, while commending the work as a "singular *jeu d'esprit,*" evidently felt its utilitarian sensibilities ruffled, objecting that "it is not for the genuine satirist, either directly, or indirectly, to insinuate the superiority of half-barbarous states of existence." It was also unhappy about Peacock's unflattering allusions to political economy in this work (1:cxl–cxli). The *Cambrian Quarterly Magazine,* which could be expected to know, described *The Misfortunes of Elphin* as "the most entertaining book, if not the best, that has yet been published on the ancient customs and traditions of Wales" (1:cxli). The *Athenaeum* was likewise favorable, while correctly predicting a small audience for the work (1:cxli–cxlii).

Modern opinion invariably sets this work over *Maid Marian,* but is less agreed on its comparative worth in relation to the novels of talk. Not as frankly topical as those more characteristic works, *The Misfortunes of Elphin* is nevertheless just as up to date in its satiric concerns, although perhaps it is less pointedly specific. It deals with issues from the broad, speculative viewpoint of the historian, rather than from the narrower, more focused one of the satirist. However, behind the historical perspective the satirist still lurks.

Boozers and bards. *The Misfortunes of Elphin* is constructed from three separate Welsh legends: the first concerns Seithenyn the Drunkard who let in the ocean upon the Plain of Gwaelod; the second, the birth of Taliesin the bard; and the third, the kidnapping of King Arthur's queen Gwenyvar by Melvas. Peacock's story opens on the reign of Gwythno Garanhir, one of a number of petty kings who ruled under the nominal sovereignty of Uther Pendragon in sixth-century Britain. Gwythno is fortunate in ruling over the Great Plain of Gwaelod, a prosperous and highly cultivated tract of land containing several thriving towns and ports, and in consequence has become a complacent and indulgent king.

Gwaelod, however, is a lowland country protected from the sea only by an embankment of "massy stone" that has stood for centuries. Busy pursuing his own pleasures, Gwythno has left the superintendence of the sea wall to a complicated bureaucracy headed by one Prince Seithenyn ap Seithyn Saidi, who is Lord High Commissioner of the Royal Embankment. An archetypally corrupt public official, Seithenyn "drank the profits, and left the embankment to his deputies, who left it to their assistants, who left it to itself" (4:5). One minor official named Teithrin does take his responsibilities seriously and is alarmed at the advanced state of dilapidation into which the embankment has fallen through the neglect of its keepers. He notifies King Gwythno's son, Prince Elphin, and together they go to see the negligent Seithenyn about it.

Seithenyn is one of the great drunkards in literature, a "Welsh Falstaff," according to his admirers.[5] Indeed, in this character Peacock at once indulges his penchants for slapstick, wine, song, and verbal sophistry. When Elphin and Teithrin enter his hall, the banqueting Seithenyn immediately displays his hospitality, if not his powers of visual discrimination, roaring, "You are welcome all four" (4:12). And yet if he is noticeably impaired in his faculties, and indeed finds himself incapable of standing to receive his guests, Seithenyn possesses amazing powers of disputation, a quality not always irreconcilable with intoxication in Peacock. With his "insane clarity of speech," as J.B. Priestly calls it,[6] Seithenyn makes an ingenious, if spurious, defense of his neglect of the seawall—"virtual superintendence" (4:10) is the political euphemism Peacock uses—exploiting the conservative appeal to "venerable antiquity" and warning against the dangers of "innovation" (4:16). The chapter ends on a typically Peacockian note of slapstick with the entire High Commission, as deeply in their cups as Seithenyn, rising in "simultaneous confusion" and abruptly joining their "fallen chief" on the floor (4:19–20).

But slapstick is followed by cataclysm, for on the night of Elphin's visit to Seithenyn a terrible sea storm breaches the wall. It destroys Seithenyn's castle and most of the inhabitants, including, it seems, Seithenyn himself. The entire Plain of Gwaelod is inundated, and King Gwythno's prosperity is at an end. A few survivors, Prince Elphin among them, escape to high ground where they eke out a subsistence.

The next part of the story concerns the birth and education of Taliesin. Elphin has become a fisherman, and one night in their salmon weir he and his wife find a basket containing a baby. They name the infant Taliesin, "radiant brow," and take him into their home. Although Peacock describes some of the Druidic mysteries into which Taliesin is initiated as a fledgling bard, Taliesin's education also recalls Anthelia Melincourt's Wordsworthian upbringing: "The youth drew in the draughts of inspiration among the mountain forests and the mountain streams, and grew up under the roof of Elphin, in the perfection of genius and beauty" (4:61). Peacock passes quickly over Taliesin's formative years. When we meet him again he is a young man and has fallen in love with Melangel, the daughter of Elphin.

The rest of the story concerns Taliesin's efforts to free Elphin, who has been kidnapped by the barbaric king Maelgon. During this quest Taliesin happens upon a miraculously resurrected Seithenyn, now a butler in the household of King Melvas, who relates how he was saved from perishing in the flood waters of Gwaelod by two providentially empty wine barrels. Taliesin also learns from this incorrigible drunkard that King Arthur's missing wife Gwenyvar is being held by Melvas. Aided (after his fashion) by Seithenyn, Taliesin manages to secure the release of Queen Gwenyvar, and Arthur, in his gratitude, compels Maelgon to free Elphin. The story ends with a Grand Bardic Congress, a kind of contest of bards, from which Taliesin emerges victorious, and with Taliesin's marriage to Melangel. Seithenyn, wily old survivor that he is, manages to obtain a place as butler in Arthur's household.

The progress of civil society.   *The Misfortunes of Elphin,* like *Maid Marian,* contains much "oblique satire" of contempory society. As in the earlier romance, this satire takes the general form of unfavorable comparisons of decadent modern man with his barbaric,

but more vital forbears. Describing a Christmas festival in chapter
12, for example, Peacock disparages Britain's "present most lugub-
rious inhabitants" and longs for a time when "England was Merry
England" (4:110). The Cymyric female, according to Peacock, is
"vigilant and energetic" (4:33), while the men are fierce hunters
and warriors. Indeed, if we disregard the irony, there is a strain in
this work that recalls Peacock's youthful Ossianic imitations with
their idealized ancient Britons.

But the irony can never be disregarded for long in Peacock.
Pointed satiric references abound in *The Misfortunes of Elphin,* and
no age, civilized or barbaric, escapes entirely unscathed, although
as always Peacock favors the Ancients over the Moderns. His comments on the factors contributing to the destruction of Gwythno's
prosperous kingdom are at once cautionary and accusing:

We, who live in more enlightened times, amidst the "gigantic strides of
intellect," when offices of public trust are so conscientiously and zealously
discharged, and so vigilantly checked and superintended, may wonder at
the wicked negligence of Seithenyn; at the sophisms with which, in his
liquor, he vindicated his system, and pronounced the eulogium of his old
dilapidations, and at the blind confidence of Gwythno and his people in
this virtual guardian of their lives and property: happy that our own public
guardians are too virtuous to act or talk like Seithenyn, and that we
ourselves are too wise not to perceive, and too free not to prevent it, if
they should be so disposed. (4:43)

In another connection Peacock notes that the songs sung by Taliesin
can yet be heard among the Welsh peasantry of the present day,
but only "on the few occasions on which rack-renting, tax-collecting,
common-enclosing, methodist-preaching, and similar developments
of the light of the age, have left them either the means or inclination
of making merry" (4:145). With its blend of irony and nostalgia,
this is a quintessentially Peacockian observation for which Peacock's
sixth-century Welsh setting provides the perfect vehicle.

Peacock's satire of the present age is developed most fully in the
section outlining Taliesin's education in chapter 6. Prefacing this
chapter with mottoes drawn from the ancient Welsh "Triads of
Wisdom"—e.g., "The three objects of intellect: the true, the beautiful, and the beneficial" (4:50)—Peacock slyly suggests how much
learning and wisdom the Ancient Welsh possessed by enumerating

all the modern learning and wisdom they lacked. Political economy, moral science, political science, steam power—all these manifestations of the "March of Mind" were unknown to them. "In short," Peacock concludes, "they made their money of metal, and breathed pure air, and drank pure water, like unscientific barbarians" (4:51). Yet, Peacock reminds us, they were still our ancestors:

> They went to work politically much as we do. The powerful took all they could get from their subjects and neighbours; and called something or other sacred and glorious, when they wanted the people to fight for them. They repressed disaffection by force, when it showed itself in an overt act; but they encouraged freedom of speech, when it was, like Hamlet's reading, "words, words, words." (4:51–52)

To Peacock, finally, human nature is essentially the same in all ages and all places. Here, as in *Maid Marian,* there is nothing new under the sun.

The Misfortunes of Elphin is Peacock's last satire of Toryism, for two years later *Crotchet Castle* would take more direct aim at the liberal "March of Mind." Marilyn Butler claims that *The Misfortunes of Elphin* is Peacock's "most political and topical book since *Melincourt,*"[7] and indeed in the venal and negligent Lord High Commissioner of the Royal Embankment we meet a Tory who would be welcome at Mainchance Villa. Among many things, Prince Seithenyn is a study of the conservative mind, or rather of one particular type of conservative mind.

Like the reactionaries of *Melincourt,* Seithenyn has a horror of change, and would hold on to the obsolete forms of the past for no other reason than that they are old—and of course because he has a vested interest in retaining them. His "virtual superintendence" (which is to say no superintendence) of the seawall depends on the arguments he puts forth in chapter 2 in justification of his negligence. These arguments generally recall Edmund Burke's defense of the existing British constitution and his warnings against those who would disturb centuries of venerable tradition with their meddling reforms. Specifically, Seithenyn may echo the speeches of George Canning (Mr. Anyside Antijack of *Melincourt*) cautioning against parliamentary reform—as Canning stated in 1821, for example, "I am not prepared to sacrifice or to hazard the fruit of

centuries of experience . . . for doubtful experiments even of possible improvement."[8] Thus if Elphin and Teithrin point out that
the embankment is in "a state of dangerous decay," Seithenyn ac-
knowledges the decay, but denies that it is dangerous. On the
contrary, the danger lies in innovation. "Our ancestors were wiser
than we," he maintains; "they built it in their wisdom; and, if we
should be so rash as to try to mend it, we should only mar it"
(4:15). The discussion that ensues is a study in the perennial opposition of reform and reaction:

> "The stonework," said Teithrin, "is sapped and mined: the piles are
> rotten, broken, and dislocated: the floodgates and sluices are leaky and
> creaky."
> "That is the beauty of it," said Seithenyn. "Some parts of it are rotten,
> and some parts of it are sound."
> "It is well," said Elphin, "That some parts are sound: it were better
> that all were so."
> "So I have heard some people say before," said Seithenyn; "perverse
> people, blind to venerable antiquity: that very unamiable sort of people,
> who are in the habit of indulging their reason. But I say, the parts that
> are rotten give elasticity to those that are sound: they give them elasticity,
> elasticity, elasticity. If it were all sound, it would break by its own
> obstinate stiffness: the soundness is checked by the rottenness, and the
> stiffness is balanced by the elasticity." (4:15—16)

Seithenyn is soon to regret his views, when, weakened by centuries
of neglect, the embankment is breached by the sea; in his cups as
always, the Lord High Commissioner of the Royal Embankment is
able only to perceive "that there was an innovation" before he is
lost in the invading waters (4:28).

The breaching of the seawall and the subsequent desolation of
Gwythno's kingdom has obvious revolutionary overtones, as many
commentators have pointed out, but this incident also carries a
historical and philosophical significance that goes beyond politics.
The inundation of Gwaelod follows in a line of similar events in
the other novels, for submersion in water seems to be a common
occurrence in Peacock. There is Mr. Cranium's near-drowning in
Headlong Hall, as well as Mr. Toobad's dunking in a moat and a
ditch in *Nightmare Abbey,* and Mr. Firedamp's in *Crotchet Castle.* As
late as *Gryll Grange* we find Lord Curryfin floundering in a lake
after a boating accident. On a larger scale, there is the great deluge

survived by Squire Headlong's ancestor on the top of Mount Snowdon and the violent mountain torrent in which Anthelia Melincourt nearly perishes. Although they vary in magnitude, all these instances describe roughly the same pattern: contentment, or complacency, followed by cataclysm, whether in the natural or the human spheres. They illustrate the inevitability of change in this world, whether for better or for worse. Such, indeed, are the reflections of Anthelia Melincourt when she finds her life threatened by a sudden mountain flood: "Though her life had been a series of uniform prosperity, she had considered deeply the changes of things, and *the nearness of the paths of night and day* in every pursuit and circumstance of human life" (2:105).

In *The Misfortunes of Elphin,* however, King Gwythno lacks the consolations of even such a philosophy. On the eve of his kingdom's destruction, ironically, Gwythno "went to sleep with a pious reflection on the goodness of Providence to himself" (4:35). In the space of a single night "The Prosperity of Gwaelod," as Peacock entitles chapter 1, is lost, and this formerly "populous and highly cultivated" plain becomes a "thinly peopled tract of rock, mountain, forest and bog," its inhabitants reduced to a few "straggling cultivators" in the highlands (4:45). Just as Voltaire found his faith in progress shattered by the terrible Lisbon earthquake of 1755, so Gwythno becomes a bitter and disappointed man following the inundation of Gwaelod. Moreover, the view of history suggested in this work is very like that to which Voltaire subscribed after Lisbon, an endless cycle of recurring periods of prosperity and ruin, "a continual alteration of day and night."[9]

And yet if the unundation has ended the prosperity of Gwaelod, it has also put an end to an old and, certainly as regards the embankment's drunken guardian Seithenyn, corrupt order. As Gwythno laments, this tragedy has been caused by "presumption, from abundance born" (4:40), like the biblical Flood. In any case, this incident drawn from Welsh mythology and surrounded by biblical overtones is curiously pertinent to Peacock's own century. Whether the inundation of Gwaelod marks the end of King Gwythno's prosperity and the beginning of Prince Elphin's misfortunes, or in more political terms the end of an old and the beginning of a new order, it clearly bears on a question debated throughout Peacock: in the words of *Crotchet Castle's* Reverend Folliot, "what is good for man in this world?" A passage in chapter 3 describing the flight of the flood survivors suggests only uncertainty and anxiety regarding man's lot:

Thus they began their march. They had not proceeded far, when the tide began to recede, the wind to abate somewhat of its violence, and the moon to look on them at intervals through the rifted clouds, disclosing the desolation of the inundated plain, silvering the tumultuous surf, gleaming on the distant mountains, and revealing a lengthened prospect of their solitary path, that lay in its irregular line like a ribbon on the deep. (4:34)

Figuring significantly in the novel is Taliesin the bard, for here, as elsewhere in Peacock, the social and political engagement of the writer is an important theme. The thesis of the ironic "Four Ages of Poetry" is that the sway of poetry has long since passed and that poets provide now only a trivial diversion. Set in sixth-century Wales, however, *The Misfortunes of Elphin* depicts a time described in "The Four Ages" when poets were the intellectual leaders of their age—its "historians . . . theologians, moralists, and legislators" (8:6). They were also venal and obsequious flatterers, and thus not so very different from many of the literary men who populate Peacock's novels of talk. Indeed, even in the age of Arthur, Taliesin is an isolated figure as he moves among the court-hirelings who constitute the literary life of sixth-century Wales. Nevertheless, he represents the light of civilization in an age when the distinction between a conquering king and a marauding bandit does not yet exist. As Marilyn Butler suggests, he embodies the ideal Poet-Legislator described in Shelley's *Defence of Poetry* (1821).[10]

It is Taliesin, significantly, who brings matters to a satisfactory conclusion in the book, not through force but politic persuasion. If poets were mankind's first legislators and moralists, Taliesin is also a very early diplomat. In chapter 14 he summons "all the energies of his genius to turn the passions of Melvas," thus gaining for Arthur both his wife and a new ally (4:133). Thus Taliesin fulfills here the first duty of the bard—and of the writer in the context of Peacock's broader concerns—which is "to animate the less-gifted multitude by examples of right conduct" (4:32). (One of Peacock's antiquarian sources for *The Misfortunes of Elphin* states that it was the duty of the primitive bard "to *enlighten* the understanding, promote *harmony* in society, and encourage virtue.")[11] This surely is also the significance of the bardic congress in chapter 15 in which Taliesin and his fellow bards perform before a—potentially at least—"candid and liberal audience" (4:135). But, as the *Athenaeum* observed in its review of *The Misfortunes of Elphin,* such an audience is elusive, it seems, even in an "enlightened" age.

Chapter Seven

Essays and Reviews: Peacock as Critic

As we might expect of a novelist in whose work opinion plays such an important role, Peacock wrote essays as well as fiction. Moreover, although they constitute a relatively small body of work, his essays and reviews make up in variety for what they lack in quantity, for they cover a surprising diversity of subjects, from steam navigation to opera, from classical drama to modern gastronomy. It could be said, indeed, that the eclecticism that characterizes Peacock the novelist likewise characterizes the essayist. His most significant essays for us are those that deal specifically with literature, primarily the unfinished "Essay on Fashionable Literature" and his best-known essay, "The Four Ages of Poetry," as well as the two essays on French comic novels. But by far the most numerous of Peacock's prose pieces are opera reviews written on a regular basis for the *Examiner* between 1829 and 1834. Peacock's interests, then, unlike those of his fictional characters, are rarely narrowly specialized, and it is this broadness of approach that his nonfictional prose shares with his fiction. For whether Peacock is writing on opera or cookery, satirizing corrupt electoral practices or landscape gardening, his abiding concern is with the sometimes very subtle but always pointed cultural and social interconnections between these subjects. To Peacock art and literature, as much as politics and economics, are intimately involved in the well-being of social man. This informing premise gives coherence to a diverse and sometimes difficult body of work.

Literary Essays

Peacock inherited from the eighteenth century not only his classicism, but his manner of viewing literature from a distinctly Enlightenment historical perspective. Like the eighteenth-century literary theorists, he believed that the literature of a society reflects that society's degree of civilization, that, along with the other arts, literature is a by-product of society.[1] Thus, according to Joseph Warton, "The manners and customs, the different ways of thinking and of living, the favourite passions, pursuits, and pleasures of men appear in no writings so strongly marked, as in the poets in their respective ages; so that in these compositions, the historian, the moralist, the politician, and the philosopher, may, each of them, meet with abundant matter for reflection and observation."[2] To the degree that a society is corrupt, then, so will its literature be debased; so far as it is healthy, so will it produce a vital, healthy literature.

Such a premise underlies the fragmentary "Essay on Fashionable Literature," in which Peacock argues that "every age has its own character, manners, and amusements, which are influenced even in their lightest forms by the fundamental features of the time" (8:265). Begun in the summer of 1818, following the completion of *Nightmare Abbey,* the essay was soon left off never to be resumed, and by the end of November Peacock wrote to Shelley informing him that he had begun to write *Maid Marian,* itself not to be completed until four years later. Written in numbered sections, the essay as it stands is obviously in an early stage of composition. Moreover, something of an imbalance in emphasis is created by a detailed defense of Coleridge's *Christabel,* which, while interesting in itself, seems a disproportionately long digression from the general account of fashionable literature opening the essay. Its flaws notwithstanding, this fragmentary piece provides an often trenchant portrait of the Regency literary world, pointedly illustrating Peacock's views on the close interrelation of literature and society.

Peacock begins by evoking the milieu of fashionable society in which move "those ornamental varieties of the human species who live to be amused for the benefit of social order" (8:263). It is a world in which novelty is the all in all, and in which books go out of fashion as swiftly as styles of dress. Hence the demand for "light and easy books which command attention without the labour of application, and amuse the idleness of fancy without disturbing the sleep of understanding" (8:263). Peacock sees in this phenomenon more than a harmless diversion, however, for the pervasiveness of "fashionable literature" he believes to be symptomatic of a general cultural malaise. Just as for *Nightmare Abbey*'s Mr. Listless the literature of the age "demonstrates the nullity of virtue and energy," so too here it only panders to apathy and triviality:

This species of literature, which aims only to amuse and must be very careful not to instruct, had never so many purveyors as at present: for there never was any state of soceity in which there were so many idle persons as there are at present in England, and it happens that these idle persons are for the most part so circumstanced that they can do nothing if they would, and in the next place that they are united in the links of a common interest which, being based in delusion, makes them even more averse than the well-dressed vulgar always are from the free exercise of reason and the bold investigation of truth. (8:263–64)

As always for Peacock, the ideal is a literature of vigorous social and intellectual engagement:

Fancy indeed treads on dangerous ground when she trespasses on the land of opinion—the soil is too slippery for her glass slippers, and the atmosphere too heavy for her filmy wings. But she is a degenerate spirit if she be contented within the limits of her own empire, and keep the mind continually gazing upon phantasms without pointing to more important realities. Her province is to awaken the mind, not to enchain it. (8:274)

Significantly, the authors invoked as exemplars of this activist literature—Cervantes, Rabelais, Swift, Voltaire, and Fielding (8:275)—are satirists to a man.

If the "Essay on Fashionable Literature" deals with modern literature as an effect of particular social circumstances, "The Four Ages of Poetry" (1820) might be said to trace the historical causes of this effect. Published in the first number of *Ollier's Literary Miscellany,* this witty essay attacking modern poetry was to have been answered by Shelley in a subsequent issue of *Ollier's.* Because no subsequent issue ever appeared, however, this reply, *A Defence of Poetry,* was not published until 1840, and in so revised a form that, as Peacock later observed, it was "a defence without an attack" (8:500).

Peacock bases his essay on a scheme of four successive ages corresponding to the metals iron, gold, silver, and brass respectively. In the age of iron, society is in its infancy and "rude bards celebrate in rough numbers the exploits of ruder chiefs" (8:3). Panegyrists by profession, then, poets are "as yet the only historians and chroniclers of their time, and the sole depositories of all the knowledge of their age" (8:6). It is a meager enough store of knowledge, "rather a crude congeries of traditional phantasies than a collection of useful truths" (8:6), and yet this is the beginning of the profession of knowledge. For while their fellow barbarians enrich themselves through sheer physical prowess, fighting and plundering, these primitive poets, venal flatterers though they are, do so by intellectual means: "Thus they sharpen their own wits and awaken those of others, at the same time that they gratify vanity and amuse curiosity" (8:6).

The age of gold that follows sees poetry in its perfection. The springs of its poetic inspiration still flow from the primitive energy and power of the iron age, while greater technical skill and knowledge are possessed by its poets. Moreover, poetry remains preeminent in the field of intellect: "It has no rivals in history, nor in philosophy, nor in science. It is cultivated by the greatest intellects of the age, and listened to by all the rest" (8:9). But gradually this preeminence begins to wane, for "new rivals arise around it in new fields of literature, which gradually acquire more influence as, with the progress of reason and civilization, facts become more interesting than fiction" (8:9).

The two ages that follow see poetry in its decline. In the age of silver, poetry becomes overrefined and derivative, "good sense and elegant learning, conveyed in polished and somewhat monotonous verse" (8:12). Worse is to come, however, for rejecting the polish and learning of the silver age, the succeeding age of brass attempts vainly to revive the age of gold. This is "the second childhood of poetry" (8:13), in which poetry becomes self-conscious and preciously archaic.

In the scheme outlined above, the iron age is termed by Peacock the "bardic," the golden the "Homeric," the silver the "Virgilian," and the brass the "Nonnic" (after an obscure late Latin poet). Modern poetry too has its four ages, moreover, which Peacock traces in the essay's second half. In this modern cycle, briefly, the Middle Ages, with its chivalric romances, corresponds to the iron age, the age of Shakespeare to the golden, the age of Pope and Dryden to the silver, and Peacock's own age, that of the romantics, to the ignominious age of brass.

It is for this latter age that the essay's harshest irony is reserved. Indeed, the account Peacock gives here of his contemporaries amounts virtually to invective:

Mr. Scott digs up the poachers and cattle-stealers of the ancient border. Lord Byron cruizes {sic} for thieves and pirates on the shores of the Morea and among the Greek islands. Mr. Southey wades through ponderous volumes of travels and old chronicles, from which he carefully selects all that is false, useless, and absurd, as being essentially poetical; and when he has a commonplace book full of monstrosities, strings them into an epic. Mr. Wordsworth picks up village legends from old women and sextons; and Mr. Coleridge, to the valuable information acquired from similiar sources, superadds the dreams of crazy theologians and the mysticism of German metaphysics, and favours the world with visions in verse, in which the quadruple elements of sexton, old woman, Jeremy Taylor, and Emanuel Kant, are harmonized into a delicious poetical compound. (8:19–20)

Nowhere else does Peacock's reputation as court jester of the Romantics seem more apt. As in the "Essay on Fashionable Literature," and in *Melincourt* and *Nightmare Abbey,* the main thrust of his attack is directed against those who have abandoned their social role as writers. Of his old foes, the Lake Poets, Peacock writes:

They wrote verses on a new principle . . . and remaining studiously ignorant of history, society, and human nature, cultivated the phantasy only at the expense of the memory and the reason; and contrived, though they had retreated from the world for the express purpose of seeing nature as she was, to see her only as she was not, converting the land they lived in into a sort of fairy-land, which they peopled with mysticisms and chimaeras. (8:18)

Thus at the essay's end Peacock envisions a great pyramid "built into the upper air of intelligence" from which mathematicians, metaphysicians, political economists, and others gaze down at the modern Parnassus below, "knowing how small a place it occupies in the comprehensiveness of their prospect" (8:25).

And yet Peacock the essayist cannot despair entirely of the role of letters in a modern age. After all, these same leaders of the "March of Mind," the philosophers, the political economists, the scientists, all are well within the scope of Peacock the satiric novelist. This is not to suggest that "The Four Ages" is finally a tract against progress, though, any more than that it is a utilitarian dismissal of poetry in the present age. With its ironically elusive manner "The Four Ages" is itself representative of the type of literature most suited to the age—polished, skeptical, as much a product of modern, polished civil society as those rational disciplines that have superseded the literature of escape and social abnegation that Peacock specifically condemns in this essay.

In 1835–36 Peacock wrote two essays for the *London Review* that, though they specifically discuss French comic literature, once again treat the interrelation of literature and society. "An intense love of truth, and a clear apprehension of truth, are both essential to comic writing of the first class" (9:262), he states in the first essay entitled "French Comic Romances" (1835). Indeed, Peacock makes large claims for comedy here:

It would be, we think, an interesting and amusing inquiry to trace the progress of French comic fiction, in its bearing on opinion, from the twelfth century to the Revolution; and to show how much this unpretending branch of literature has, by its universal diffusion through so many ages in France, contributed to directing the stream of opinion against the mass of delusions and abuses which it was the object of those who were honest in the cause of the Reformation, and in the causes of the several changes which have succeeded it to the present time, to dissipate and destroy. (9:259)

Thus it is that "among the most illustrious authors of comic fiction are some of the most illustrious specimens of political honesty and heroic self-devotion" (9:261). As he wrote this, Peacock might have been recalling the militant motto of the earlier *Melincourt*—*Vocem Commoedia Tollit* (Comedy raises its voice)—and with just satisfaction, for that satire of political imposture was published in a year of harsh government repression when prominent radicals such as William Cobbett were fleeing the country. Nearly two decades later the radical associate of Shelley is still recognizable.

Peacock distinguishes two classes of comic fiction in "French Comic Romances": that in which opinion predominates, characters being merely a means of embodying opinion; and that in which character is central and opinions incidental. It is the absence of the first class of literature in his age—a category to which his own earlier novels quite clearly belong—that Peacock laments in his second *London Review* article "The Epicier" (1836). *Epicier* is French for "grocer," but, as Carl Dawson points out, it carries the broader sense here of "philistine."[3] For Peacock, indeed, it is the age of the *épicier*: "The *épicier* votes—the *épicier* elects; the *épicier* does not discuss, but the *épicier* decides, and the *épicier* administers" (9:310). What Peacock is criticizing here is the tyranny of a narrow and unreflecting dogmatism that he associates with the commercial petite bourgeoisie. It is no accident that the forum is an identifying feature of Peacock's fiction, is indeed both a literary and social ideal, and it is such intellectual engagement that modern literature lacks, in Peacock's view: "Among a people disposed to think, their everyday literature will bear the impress of thought; among a people not so disposed, the absence or negation of thought will be equally conspicuous in their literature" (9:294).

Although he wrote few literary reviews, Peacock could be formidable when he did. The broad cultural concerns of "The Four Ages" and the *London Review* essays are absent here, however, and Peacock's criticisms seem narrower in their scope, even idiosyncratic on occasion. In the *Westminster Review* for October 1827 he wrote a scathing review of Thomas Moore's novel *The Epicurean,* which work he found to have no artistic merits whatsoever, "poetical, descriptive, narrative, or dramatic" (9:67). Worse, Moore seems to have had no very historical sense of his subject, for which Peacock (who had little more in his own *Maid Marian*) trounces him: "Mr. Moore has misrepresented the Epicurean philosophy, and the character of the later Epicureans. He has drawn an Epicurean according to the vulgar notion entertained of that character by persons who know nothing about the matter" (9:46). Another review of Moore, this time concerning the first volume of his *Letters and Journals of Lord Byron,* is no more favorable. Alarmed by these attacks, Moore persuaded the editors of the *Westminster* to restrain Peacock from reviewing the second volume.

The essays of Peacock's later years are by contrast much more appreciative in their manner and tone. Appearing in *Fraser's Magazine* in 1858, "Chapelle and Bachaumont" is a good-natured account of two minor French authors. *Horae Dramaticae* is a series of essays on the classical drama. These pieces on *Querolus* (a Latin comedy), Euripides' *Phaëthon,* and Cratinus's *The Flask* are informal, though informed, introductions, "not following any order of chronology or classification," as Peacock states, "but only that in which our readings or reminiscences may suggest them" (10:4).

Biographical Essays

If Peacock the essayist sheds some light on Peacock the novelist, Peacock the man remains elusive in his essays. In an age of great autobiographical essayists such as William Hazlitt, Charles Lamb, and Thomas De Quincey, and of letter-writers such as John Keats and Lord Byron, Peacock maintains an eighteenth-century reserve. His letters are disappointingly scanty and desultory,[4] while the only diary he is known to have kept covers barely two months in 1818, and that at any rate is a record of only the most superficial events of Peacock's daily life. His nonfictional prose does include a few autobiographical pieces, however, and his Shelley memoirs are interesting not only for their portrait of Shelley but for what they reveal—little enough, perhaps—about Peacock himself and his friendship with the poet.

Peacock in fact wrote his "Memoirs of Percy Bysshe Shelley" reluctantly, as a corrective to the several lives of Shelley that had begun to appear, notably Thomas Jefferson Hogg's self-serving biography of the poet. Written in installments in *Fraser's Magazine* in 1859 and 1860, the "Memoirs," then, are essentially Peacock's attempt to set the record straight. Indeed, the first article opens with a general denunciation of the vogue for biography. "It is the old village scandal on a larger scale," Peacock says, "and as in these days of universal locomotion people know nothing of their neighbours, they prefer tittle-tattle about notorieties to the retailing of whispers about the Jenkinses and Tomkinses of the vicinity" (8:39). But while Peacock believed that "no man is bound to write the life of another" (8:40), he felt bound to defend the memory of his friend from misconstruction, whether that of exploitive biographers like Hogg or of Victorian polemicists who found in the life and opinions of the dead poet grist for their particular mills, religious and political, and the "Memoirs" offer a balanced, if brief and restrained, account of the poet. Otherwise, Peacock states, he would have preferred that Shelley "had been allowed to remain a voice and a mystery: that, like his own Skylark, he had been left unseen in his congenial region" (8:42).

Perhaps the most sensitive aspect of Shelley's life addressed by Peacock concerns Harriet Shelley, whom Shelley abandoned for Mary Godwin. Without vindicating or condemning either Harriet or Shelley, Peacock simply presents the facts of this sad episode as he understood them. Similarly, his discussion of Shelley's tendency toward romantic self-dramatization is neither credulous nor patronizing. His reminiscences are not without warmth, however, and he relates several anecdotes with a gentle humor that reveals his fondness for Shelley, and, moreover—rare in accounts of the poet—

credits Shelley himself with a sense of humor (8:113). At a time
when Shelley was a subject of intensely partisan debate, biographical
and political, Peacock is concerned in this brief, restrained account
to avoid any riding of personal hobbyhorses, and to present a credible
portrait of his old friend.

Peacock wrote two other essays, which, autobiographical in nature, might be compared to Charles Lamb's essays in their nostalgic
retrospection. "Recollections of Childhood: the Abbey House," appearing in 1837 in *Bentley's Miscellany,* is a brief piece in which
Peacock recalls the household of an old childhood friend. He describes in fond detail both the abbey house and its "amiable, simple-
mannered, old English inhabitants" (8:29), although even here he
manages a few sidelong satiric glances at the modern "march of
mind" that has brought an end to the manner of living celebrated
in the essay. "The Last Day of Windsor Forest" was probably drafted
in 1862, but remained unpublished until after Peacock's death. It
is written in much the same strain as the earlier "Abbey House."
Here Peacock recalls Windsor Forest—now enclosed—as he knew
it as a young man, and his final statement on the inevitable changes
that have transformed this particular place, and indeed all other
places, suggests the stoical resignation of old age: "So be it" (8:149).

Miscellaneous Essays

Apart from his writings on music, and specifically on the opera,
Peacock's other prose writings fall into no readily defined classes.
They include a technical article published in an issue of the 1835
Edinburgh Review on steam navigation, a subject in which Peacock
could claim considerable expertise, having been actively involved
in the development and use of steamships in the East India Company's fleet. Peacock's still-vigorous, if by this time tempered, liberalism is evident in his enthusiastic review of Thomas Jefferson's
memoirs in the *Westminster Review* for 1830. Indeed, in the encom-
ium that concludes this piece Peacock might be describing the liberal
knight-errant on whom Anthelia Melincourt has set her heart: "Such
a rare combination of an enthusiasm almost chivalrous for the liberty
and happiness of mankind, with a calm philosophical judgment,
restraining its pursuits within the limits of the attainable; such a
picture of political sincerity, presenting always the same character
in appearance as in reality, in public as in private life" (9:185).

Appearing the same year as "Jefferson's Memoirs" in the *Westminster Review,* "London Bridge" inevitably prompts comparisons with Prince Seithenyn's sophistical arguments against "innovation" in *The Misfortunes of Elphin.* Peacock, however, demonstrates a mastery of technical detail in his argument against replacing the ancient bridge with a modern structure that Seithenyn could never manage. As in his fictionalized debates, he sets pro against con, fact against fact, here to arrive at the conclusion that a change would not be for the best, might indeed be for the worst. Envisioning flooding as a possible consequence, Peacock reverts momentarily to the slapstick of his novels:

Logs of mahogany will swim about Bankside; kitchen-fires will be extinguished in Lambeth; cabbages will be submerged, and melon-frames floated off at Millbank; the Duchess of Buccleugh's beautiful villa at Richmond, will become a 'house of pleasaunce' for Naiads: and our two-tailed friends will be set paddling about Westminster Hall, and sending forth sounds as choral, though not as musical, as those which Aristophanes puts into the mouths of the Frogs of the Styx. (9:206)

Moreover, behind even the impressive marshalling of relevant facts throughout the essay is Peacock's temperamental preference for things past. "We do not like these sweeping changes," he confesses at the essay's end, "which . . . obliterate every visible sign that connects the present generation with the ages that are gone" (9:219).

During the late 1820s and early 1830s Peacock wrote a considerable body of music reviews, mainly on the opera, for the *Globe* and the *Examiner.* His novels abound with musical references, many of which are specifically operatic, and Peacock is thought to have introduced Shelley to the opera, so this stint as music reviewer was the fruit of an enthusiasm cultivated for many years. Peacock is a knowledgeable and appreciative reviewer, if peevishly crotchety on such subjects as noisy audiences and hats that obstruct the stage— "those walls of gauze, lace, silk, velvet, or plumage, which some women, with a selfish disregard of the comfort of others, are in the habit of building on their heads" (9:406). Conductors who rap their batons too loudly—"he does not beat time; he threshes it" (9:407)— and incompetent stage managers are frequently singled out for censure. A more serious criticism concerns the careless alteration of operas. Of one production, for example, Peacock observes that it was "made up apparently by picnic from the portmanteaus of the performers, with a *libretto* put together by the printers' devil, in which one thing was read while another was sung" (9:421). Peacock could be warmly appreciative, however, particularly of performances that in his view demonstrated genuine "feeling" as opposed to mere brilliance of execution, a preference voiced in his fiction as well. Besides these brief reviews and notices, he wrote two more lengthy pieces on the opera, a review of Lord Mount-Edgcumbe's *Musical Reminiscences* and an essay on the operatic composer Bellini, both for the *London Review* in 1835.

Cookery is as much a preoccupation in Peacock's fiction as music, and fittingly his essays include a piece entitled "Gastronomy and Civilization." Published in an 1851 issue of *Fraser's Magazine,* this essay bears the initials of Mary Meredith, but it is likely the product of a collaboration between Peacock and his daughter for which Peacock may take the major credit. The essay might be more appropriately entitled "Gastronomy and Literature," for its authorities are mainly literary, the progress of cookery from Homer to Voltaire (although this same year Peacock also began working on an actual cook book, "The Science of Cookery," which he unfortunately never completed). "Gastronomy and Civilization," however, is an erudite and witty survey of cooking down the ages. Some points made in this essay, such as the observation that "we have brought chemistry into our kitchens, not as a handmaid but as a poisoner" (9:394), retain their trenchant relevance today. For Peacock, indeed, there is no subject that does not touch in some way on the social good.

Chapter Eight

Conclusion

"In the questions which have come within my scope," Peacock wrote to his friend Thomas L'Estrange in 1861, "I have endeavoured to be impartial, and to say what could be said on both sides" (8:253). Indeed, at times in his satire Peacock seems to have succeeded so well in being impartial as to be rather difficult to pin down on particular questions. However, far from dwelling exclusively among the "doubts and negations" to which James Spedding relegated him, Peacock observed his age from a distinct and consistent vantage ground—that of the committed and engaged critic of society. If what he observed in his age was itself rarely distinct or consistent, this is another matter; that he refused to evade such ambiguity is surely a strength in his satire.

Certainly, there is no denying that Peacock's country-house controversies present a bewildering scene. Fashionable novelists, periodical reviewers, painters, landscapers, phrenologists, transcendentalists, musicians, poets, political economists, ichthyologists, astrologers, toxicologists, medievalists, geographers, meteorologists: they are a diverse party, and a slyly comic demonstration of Adam Smith's doctrine of the "division of labour." Their various intellectual obsessions are monstrous instances of modern specialization, the consequences of the process described in "The Four Ages of Poetry" when poetry, once preeminent in the field of intellect, wanes, and "new rivals arise around it in new fields." And yet behind the factious and seemingly inconclusive dinner debates that occupy these characters is Peacock's "invisible hand," selecting and positioning, even, on occasion, applauding—though one must listen closely for this.

But where precisely do Peacock's beliefs lie? Can we properly speak of any sort of coherent philosophy or creed underlying his satire? In a discussion of Manicheanism—an early, dualistic Christian heresy that represented Satan as coeternal with God—John Stuart Mill observed:

A creed like this, which I have known to be devoutly held by at least one cultivated and conscientious person of our own day, allows it to be believed that all the mass of evil which exists was undesigned by, and exists not only by the appointment of, but in spite of the Being whom we are called upon to worship. A virtuous human being assumes in this theory the exalted character of a fellow-labourer with the Highest, a fellow-combatant in the great strife; contributing his little, which by the aggregation of many like himself becomes much, towards that progressive ascendancy, and ultimately complete triumph of good over evil. [1]

The "cultivated and conscientious person" is Mill's father, James Mill, but this account might equally apply to a colleague of both Mills at the India House—namely, Thomas Love Peacock. While it is difficult to credit Peacock with a "devoutly held" creed of any kind, it is possible that if he could be said to have had a creed it was very like that one described by Mill here.

Peacock's fragmentary Zoroastrian epic, "Ahrimanes," is the most explicit indication of this Manichean habit of mind, with its opposing principles of light and darkness, good and evil, and its premise—unrealized in the poem as it stands—of an eventual victory for the forces of light. But even in the comic turn that is given this scheme in *Headlong Hall,* where the eternal powers of darkness and light are replaced by a group of nineteenth-century dilettanti debating the pros and cons of progress, there is the same conviction that "light" will ultimately prevail, if only in the conventionally comic affirmation of civil society provided in the multiple marriages that close the novel. Perhaps nowhere else is Peacock more obviously a "fellow-combatant in the great strife" than in *Melincourt.* In a speech urging the effectiveness of "individual example" this novel's hero, Mr. Forester, adapts Homer's allegory of the two urns, one of good and one of evil. Every individual has at birth a phial holding one drop of liquid, which will be evil if poured into the urn of evil, and good if poured into the urn of good. Does the wise man follow the example of the generality of men, and pour his phial into the urn of evil?

No: you would rather say, "That neglected urn contains the hopes of the human species: little, indeed, is the addition I can make to it, but it will be good as far as it goes;" and if, on approaching the urn, you should find it not so empty as you had anticipated, if the genius appointed to guard it should say to you, "There is enough in this urn already to allow a reasonable expectation that it will one day be full, and yet it has only accumulated drop by drop through the efforts of individuals, who broke through the pale and pressure of the multitude, and did not despair of human virtue," would you not feel ten thousand times repaid for the difficulties you had overcome, and the scoffs of the fools and slaves you had abandoned, by the single reflection that would then rush upon your mind, *I am one of these?* (2:48)

This sanguine creed of engagement informs Peacock's other novels as well. The forces of cheerfulness battle those of gloom in *Nightmare Abbey,* where the optimistic Mr. Hilary urges us "to preserve and improve all that is good, and destroy or alleviate all that is evil" (3:109). "On the whole," observes Reverend Opimian in *Gryll Grange,* "I agree in opinion with Theseus, that there is more good than evil in the world" (5:63). Indeed, arising from the heated, but rarely vituperative, debates that animate the novels there is, finally, this sense that some progress toward "light," a synthesis of seemingly irreconcilable viewpoints, is not only possible, but perhaps imminent even in the midst of conflict. Hence the bond of social union achieved at least momentarily among such sundry antithetical types as a high Anglican Tory, an Owenite cooperationalist, a political economist, and a medieval antiquarian at the end of *Crotchet Castle.* There are, of course, no clear-cut answers; often, Peacock's discordant dinner debates seem no more consequential than the repasts that occasion them. Yet, the tenacity with which they are pursued by Peacock and his obsessed disputants is surely redeeming in itself. Even at his most equivocal, Peacock reveals in his debates a genuine engagement with ideas and a commitment to the dialectical processes that shape these ideas and ultimately reconcile them with each other. "If he produce but a single volume consecrated to moral truth, its effect must be good as far as it goes" observes *Melincourt*'s Mr. Forester of the engaged writer, and Peacock claims no more or less for himself, working within the constraints of his particular art and of his particular creed.

It is, perhaps, these self-imposed constraints that have limited his subsequent appeal and influence. Possible literary antecedents notwithstanding, Peacock's novels are nothing if not characteristic, and for that reason they are highly imitable but not truly influential. Peacock has had his imitators. The most obvious of these, W. H. Mallock, published in 1877 *The New Republic,* a Victorian reworking of the Peacockian formula, with crotcheteers based on such contemporary notables as Matthew Arnold and Walter Pater. However, if Peacock could be said to have influenced any important writer in his own century, it is his son-in-law George Meredith. Meredith's famous "Essay on Comedy" affirms the role of ideas in fiction, and in his novels intellectualism constantly mixes with farce. Certain of Meredith's dinner conversations, indeed, clearly recall the talkative banquets in Peacock. Character is much more developed in Meredith than in Peacock, and, though in this respect Meredith works in the realistic mode of mainstream English fiction, his novels are at the same time more conceptually than organically structured. Meredith's fictional legacy, then, his highly patterned comedy, and his intellectualism—qualities so anomalous in nineteenth-century fiction, if somewhat less so now—is also Peacock's legacy.

The novelist of this century who most resembles Peacock in his fictional form is Aldous Huxley. Huxley's first novel, *Chrome Yellow* (1921), comes complete with a country house, plenty of talk, and opinionated guests, some of them based on famous contemporaries of Huxley like Bertrand Russell. His later novels, such as *Brave New World* (1932) and *Eyeless in Gaza* (1936), are not obviously Peacockian in provenance, although they bear Peacock's imprint in their preoccupation with ideas and in their manner of developing character and action out of the incessant clash of these ideas. Other modern novelists could be cited who owe a debt, direct or indirect, to Peacock: Norman Douglas, for example, in whose *South Wind* (1917) the country house is replaced by an island—as well, to a lesser extent, as Ronald Firbank and Evelyn Waugh. A host of more recent comic novelists like Thomas Pynchon and John Barth have pushed Peacock's intellectual anarchism to its limits. What all these writers share with Peacock is a conception of the novel that challenges our rather confined expectations as to what the novel is and what it should do. Ideas, individually and collectively, are its dynamics; it is detached and iconoclastic, and perhaps for this reason Peacock is now beginning to find the sympathetic readership his friend Shelley predicted for him:

> His fine wit
> Makes such a wound, the knife is lost in it;
> A strain too learned for a shallow age,
> Too wise for selfish bigots—let his page

Which charms the chosen spirits of the time
Fold itself up for the serener clime
Of years to come, and find its recompense
In that just expectation.[2]

Notes and References

Preface

1. James Spedding, "Tales by the Author of *Headlong Hall*," *Edinburgh Review* 68 (January 1839):443.
2. A. E. Dyson, "Peacock: The Wand of Enchantment" in *The Crazy Fabric: Essays in Irony* (London: Macmillan, 1956), 62. See also Mario Praz, *The Hero in Eclipse in Victorian Fiction,* trans. Angus Davidson (Toronto: University of Toronto Press, 1956); and Humphrey House, "The Works of Peacock," *Listener* 42 (8 December 1949):997–98.
3. Marilyn Butler, *Peacock Displayed: A Satirist in his Context* (Boston: Routledge & Kegan Paul, 1979), ix.
4. House, "Works of Peacock," 144.

Chapter One

1. Virginia Woolf, "How Should One Read a Book?" *The Common Reader* (London: Hogarth Press, 1932), 263.
2. *The Halliford Edition of the Works of Thomas Love Peacock,* ed. H. F. B. Brett-Smith and C. E. Jones (New York: AMS Press, 1967), 1:1. Further quotations from Peacock's works will be taken from this edition, and cited parenthetically in the text by volume and page number.
3. House, "Works of Peacock," 998.
4. *The Letters of Percy Bysshe Shelley,* ed. F. L. Jones (Oxford: Oxford University Press, 1964), 1:380.
5. J. B. Priestley, *Thomas Love Peacock* (New York: St. Martin's Press, 1966), 21.
6. Quoted by Carl Van Doren, *The Life of Thomas Love Peacock* (New York: Russell & Russell, 1966), 60.
7. *Letters of . . . Shelley,* 1:380.
8. Ibid., 1:392.
9. Quoted by Eleanor Nicholes, "Thomas Love Peacock," *Shelley and his Circle* (Cambridge, Mass.: Harvard University Press, 1961), 1:101.
10. Percy Bysshe Shelley, "Letter to Maria Gisborne," *The Complete Works of Percy Bysshe Shelley,* ed. R. Ingpen and Walter E. Peck (New York: Gordian Press, 1965), 4:9.
11. Nicholes, "Thomas Love Peacock," 1:104
12. Robert Buchanan, "Thomas Love Peacock: A Personal Reminiscence," *New Quarterly Magazine* 4 (April, 1875):241.

Chapter Two

1. For a comprehensive and judicious survey of Peacock's poetry see Carl Dawson, *His Fine Wit: A Study of Thomas Love Peacock* (London: Routledge & Kegan Paul, 1970), 9–70.

2. Priestley, 113.

3. Quoted by Martin Freeman, *Thomas Love Peacock: A Critical Study* (London: Martin Secker, 1911), 37.

4. Dawson, *His Fine Wit*, 20.

5. Felix Felton, *Thomas Love Peacock* (London: Allen & Unwin, 1973), 43.

6. *Letters of . . . Shelley*, 1:325.

7. *Eighteenth-Century Literature*, Geoffrey Tillotson et al., eds., (New York: Harcourt, Brace & World, 1960), 785n.

8. *Letters of . . . Shelley*, 1:325.

9. Butler, *Peacock Displayed*, 28.

10. William Wordsworth, "Preface to the Second Edition of the Lyrical Ballads (1800)," *English Romantic Writers*, ed. David Perkins (New York: Harcourt Brace Jovanovich, 1967), 328.

11. Quoted by Dawson, *His Fine Wit*, 35.

12. *Letters of . . . Shelley*, 1:569.

13. Butler, *Peacock Displayed*, 107.

14. *Letters of . . . Shelley*, 2:126.

Chapter Three

1. Howard Mills, *Peacock: his Circle and his Age* (Cambridge: Cambridge University Press, 1969), 1.

2. Ibid.

3. Joseph Warton, *An Essay on the Genius and Writings of Pope* (New York: Garland Publishing, 1970), 2:262;1:135.

4. Ibid., 1:211.

5. Thomas Warton, *The History of English Poetry* (London: J. Dodsley, 1775), 3:500.

6. Frances Russell quoted by Dawson, *His Fine Wit*, 162.

7. Priestley, *Peacock*, 144.

8. George Meredith, *An Essay on Comedy and the Uses of the Comic Spirit* (London: Constable, 1919), 8.

9. *Letters of . . . Shelley*, 1:25.

10. Lord Monboddo (James Burnet), *Of the Origin and Progress of Language* (Menston: Scolar Press, 1967), 4:308–9.

11. Ibid., 4:344.

12. Dawson, *His Fine Wit*, 164–66. See also Hakan Kjellin, *Talkative Banquets* (Stockholm: Almqvist & Wiksell, 1974).

13. Northrop Frye, *Anatomy of Criticism: Four Essays* (Princeton: Princeton University Press, 1971), 309.

14. Ibid., 311.

15. Dawson, *His Fine Wit,* 164.

16. Quoted by Lorna Sage, ed., *Peacock: the Satirical Novels: a Casebook* (London: Macmillan, 1976), 53.

17. Mills, *Peacock: his Circle and his Age,* 84.

18. Van Doren, *Peacock,* 81.

19. Dawson, *His Fine Wit,* 182.

20. For an account of this strain in literature see Lois Whitney, *Primitivism and the Idea of Progress in Popular Literature of the Eighteenth Century* (New York: Octagon Books, 1965).

21. Adam Ferguson, *An Essay on the History of Civil Society* (Edinburgh: Edinburgh University Press, 1966), 244.

22. See Butler, *Peacock Displayed,* 57.

23. William Godwin, *An Enquiry Concerning Political Justice,* ed. F. E. L. Priestley (Toronto: University of Toronto Press, 1946), 2:135.

24. Ibid., 2:535; Jean Jacques Rousseau, "Discourse on the Origin and Foundations of Inequality," *The Social Contract and Discourses,* trans. G. D. H. Cole (London: Everyman's Library, 1963), 170.

25. Quoted by Christopher Hussey, *The Picturesque: Studies in Point of View* (London: G. P. Putnam's Sons, 1972), 144.

26. Butler sees what happens in chapter 8 as a "central symbol for the tastelessness, pointlessness and extravagance of advanced society": *Peacock Displayed,* 46.

27. Rousseau, "Discourse on . . . Inequality," 167.

28. Constantine François Chasseboeuf Volney, *The Ruins: or Meditation on the Revolutions of Empires* (New York: Calvin Blanchard, n.d.), 65.

Chapter Four

1. *Letters of . . . Shelley,* 1:518.

2. Ibid., 2:244.

3. Priestley, *Peacock,* 36.

4. Quoted by Van Doren, *Peacock,* 92–93.

5. According to Howard Mills, "there is something false and forced about Peacock's attempt at close intellectual sympathy with Shelley the 'enemy to every shape of tyranny and superstitious imposture' ": *Peacock: his Circle and his Age,* 97.

6. Butler, *Peacock Displayed,* 68.

7. Brett-Smith argues that the printers found the novel in its original form to be too long for a single volume, and too short for three (1:lxx–lxxi).

8. Godwin, *Political Justice*, 2:454–55.

9. "Parliamentary Reform," *Quarterly Review* 16 (October 1816):226.

10. Ibid., 253.

11. Ibid.

12. *Letters of . . . Shelley*, 2:27.

13. Ibid., 1:574.

14. Kenneth Neill Cameron also discusses what he calls Shelley's tendency toward "morbid self-dramatization" in *The Young Shelley: Genesis of a Radical* (London: Victor Gollancz, 1951), 237.

15. Butler, *Peacock Displayed*, 135.

16. *Complete Works of . . . Shelley*, 1:241.

17. Ibid., 1:xi.

18. Mills, *Peacock: his Circle and his Age*, 163.

19. In a letter dated 16 August 1818, Shelley writes, *"Nightmare Abbey* finished. Well, what is in it? What is it? You are as secret as if the priest of Ceres had dictated its sacred pages. However, I suppose I shall see in time": *Letters of . . . Shelley*, 2:29.

20. Ibid., 2:98.

Chapter Five

1. Butler, *Peacock Displayed*, 183.

2. J. B. Priestley, for example, believes *Crotchet Castle* to be the "richest and ripest" of all Peacock's novels, whereas A. E. Dyson finds it to be the "harshest and least pleasing": Priestley, *Peacock*, 73; Dyson, *The Crazy Fabric*, 67.

3. Butler, *Peacock Displayed*, 183.

4. Robert Southey, *Sir Thomas More: or, Colloquies on the Progress and Prospects of Society* (London: J. Murray, 1829), 1:79.

5. Butler, *Peacock Displayed*, 206–7.

6. Robert Owen, *A New View of Society {and} Report to the County of Lanark*, ed. V. A. C. Gatrell (Harmondsworth: Penguin books, 1970), 220.

7. Ibid., 239.

8. Lionel Madden, *Thomas Love Peacock* (London: Evans Brothers, 1967), 133.

9. John Stuart Mill, "The Utility of Religion," *Three Essays on Religion* (London: Longman's, Green, Reader, & Dyer, 1874), 103.

10. Van Doren, *Peacock*, 245.

11. Katherine H. Porter, *Through a Glass Darkly: Spiritualism in the Browning Circle* (New York: Octagon Books, 1972), 136.

12. John Henry Newman, *The Idea of a University* (Garden City: Image Books, 1959), 163.

13. Ibid.

Chapter Six

1. Joseph Ritson, *Robin Hood: A Collection of all the Ancient Poems, Songs, and Ballads* (London: T. Egerton, 1795), 1:xii.
2. Eric J. Hobsbawm *Primitive Rebels: Studies in Archaic Forms of Social Movement in the 19th and 20th Centuries* (Manchester, England: Manchester University Press, 1959), 20–21.
3. Dawson, *His Fine Wit,* 240.
4. See Herbert Wright, "The Associations of Thomas Love Peacock with Wales," *Essays and Studies by Members of the English Association* (Oxford: Clarendon Press, 1926) 12:24–46.
5. Olwen W. Campbell, *Thomas Love Peacock* (London: Arthur Barker, 1953), 63.
6. Priestley, *Peacock,* 186.
7. Butler, *Peacock Displayed,* 160.
8. Quoted by William Hazlitt, "Table Talk," *The Complete Works of William Hazlitt,* ed. P. P. Howe (London: J. M. Dent, 1931), 8:153.
9. Roland N. Stromberg, *An Intellectual History of Modern Europe* (Englewood Cliffs, N.J.: Prentice-Hall, 1975), 142.
10. Butler, *Peacock Displayed,* 174.
11. Edward Davies, *Celtic Researches* (London: J. Booth, 1804), 170.

Chapter Seven

1. In this connection see Butler's chapter on Peacock's criticism: *Peacock Displayed,* 272–313.
2. Warton, *Essay on the Genius and Writings of Pope,* 1:348.
3. Dawson, *His Fine Wit,* 106.
4. To date, the Halliford Peacock contains the best selection of Peacock's letters, but a much fuller edition of the letters is presently being compiled by Professor Nicholas Joukovsky of Pennsylvania State University.

Chapter Eight

1. Mill, *Three Essays on Religion,* 116–17.
2. "Letter to Maria Gisborne," *Complete Works of . . . Shelley,* 4:9–10.

Selected Bibliography

1. Novels
Crotchet Castle. London: T. Hookham Jr., 1831.
Gryll Grange. London: Parker, Son, & Bourn, 1861. (published serially
    in *Fraser's Magazine,* April 1860–December 1860)
Headlong Hall. London: T. Hookham Jr. and E. T. Hookham, 1816.
Maid Marian. London: T. Hookham Jr. and Longman, Hurst, Rees, Orme,
    & Brown, 1822.
Melincourt. 3 vols. London: T. Hookham Jr. and Baldwin, Craddock, &
    Joy, 1817.
The Misfortunes of Elphin. London: T. Hookham Jr., 1829.
Nightmare Abbey. London: T. Hookham Jr. and Baldwin, Craddock, &
    Joy, 1818.

2. Poetry
The Genius of the Thames: A Lyrical Poem, in Two Parts. London: T. Hookham
    Jr. and E. T. Hookham, 1810.
The Monks of St. Mark. London, 1804.
Palmyra, and Other Poems. London: T. Bensley, 1806.
Paper Money Lyrics and Other Poems. London: C. and W. Reynell, 1837.
The Philosophy of Melancholy, a Poem in Four Parts with a Mythological Ode.
    London: T. Hookham Jr. and E. T. Hookham; Edinburgh: John
    Ballantyne, 1812.
Rhododaphne: or The Thessalian Spell, a Poem. London: T. Hookham Jr. and
    E. T. Hookham, 1818.
The Round Table; or, King Arthur's Feast. London: John Arliss, 1817.
Sir Proteus: A Satirical Ballad, by P. M. O'Donovan, Esq. London:
    T. Hookham Jr. and E. T. Hookham, 1814.

3. Collected Works
The Halliford Edition of the Works of Thomas Love Peacock. Edited by H. F.
    B. Brett-Smith and C. E. Jones. 10 vols. London: Constable, 1924–
    1934; New York: AMS Press, 1967.

4. Selected Editions
Memoirs of Shelley and other Essays and Reviews. Edited by Howard Mills.
    London: Rupert Hart-Davies, 1970.

Nightmare Abbey {and} Crotchet Castle. Edited by Raymond Wright. Harmondsworth: Penguin, 1969.

The Novels of Thomas Love Peacock. Edited by David Garnett. 2 vols. London: Rupert Hart-Davis, 1963.

The Works of Thomas Love Peacock, including his novels, poems, fugitive pieces, criticisms, etc. Edited by Henry Cole. 3 vols. London: Richard Bentley & Son, 1875.

5. Correspondence

To date, the Halliford edition provides the most substantial selection of Peacock's letters. A complete edition of the collected letters is currently being prepared by Professor Nicholas Joukovsky of Pennsylvania State university.

SECONDARY SOURCES

1. Bibliographies

Read, Bill. "Thomas Love Peacock: An Enumerative Bibliography." *Bulletin of Bibliography* 24 (September–December, 1963):32–34; (January–April, 1964):70–72; (May-August, 1964):88–91.

Ward, William S. "Contemporary Reviews of Thomas Love Peacock: A Supplementary List for the Years 1805–1820." *Bulletin of Bibliography* 25 (1967 January–April):35.

Madden, Lionel. "A Short Guide to Peacock Studies." *Critical Survey* 4 (Summer, 1970):193–97.

2. Books and Parts of Books

Able, Augustus Henry. *George Meredith and Thomas Love Peacock: A Study in Literary Influence.* Philadelphia: University of Philadelphia Press, 1933. Useful for its comments on Peacock as well as for what it has to say about Peacock's influence on Meredith.

Burns, Bryan. *The Novels of Thomas Love Peacock.* London: Croom Helm, 1985. Offers a close reading of Peacock's fiction.

Bush, Douglas. *Mythology and the Romantic Tradition in English Poetry.* Cambridge, Mass.: Harvard University Press, 1937. One of the few important discussions of Peacock's poetry, with emphasis on *Rhododaphne.*

Butler, Marilyn. *Peacock Displayed: A Satirist in his Context.* Boston: Routledge & Kegan Paul, 1979. An excellent study of Peacock's works against their original intellectual, political, and social background.

Campbell, Olwen Ward. *Thomas Love Peacock*. London: Arthur Barker, 1953. A brief and perceptive survey of Peacock's life and works.

Dawson, Carl. *His Fine Wit: A Study of Thomas Love Peacock*. London: Routledge & Kegan Paul, 1970. Perhaps the most comprehensive study of Peacock. Considers in great detail the nonfictional prose and the poetry as well as the fiction.

————. *Thomas Love Peacock*. Profiles in Literature. London: Routledge & Kegan Paul, 1968. Very brief introduction.

Dyson, A. E. "Peacock: The Wand of Enchantment." *The Crazy Fabric*. London: Macmillan, 1956. Critical, but judicious consideration of Peacock as a comic artist.

Freeman, Alexander Martin. *Thomas Love Peacock: A Critical Study*. London: Martin Secker, 1911. Diffusely written, but still useful early study.

Jack, Ian. "Peacock." *English Literature, 1815–1832*. Oxford: Oxford University Press, 1965. Balanced and concise account of Peacock as novelist and poet.

Keats-Shelley Memorial Bulletin 36 (1985). Special issue on Peacock with articles by Nicholas Joukovsky, Lionel Madden, Marilyn Butler, Howard Mills, Bryan Burns, and Carl Dawson.

Kjellin, Hakan. *Talkative Banquets*. Stockholm: Almqvist & Wiksell, 1974. A discussion of structure in the novels. Especially good on Peacock's use of the dialogue form.

Madden, Lionel. *Thomas Love Peacock*. London: Evans Bros., 1967. An excellent brief introduction to Peacock.

Mayoux, Jean-Jacques. *Un Epicurien anglais: Thomas Love Peacock*. Paris: Librairie Nizet & Bastard, 1933. Encyclopedic in scope, this study remains untranslated.

Mills, Howard. *Peacock: his Circle and his Age*. Cambridge: Cambridge University Press, 1969. Considers only the first three novels. Good discussions of Peacock in relation to such contemporaries as Shelley, Coleridge, Hazlitt, and Byron.

Praz, Mario. "Thomas Love Peacock." *The Hero in Eclipse in Victorian Fiction*. Toronto: University of Toronto Press, 1956. Unsympathetic but provocative discussion.

Priestley, J. B. *Thomas Love Peacock*. New York: Macmillan, 1927. Still among the most perceptive and best-written discussions of Peacock.

Sage, Lorna, ed. *Peacock: the Satirical Novels*. New York: Longmans, Green & Co., 1976. A compilation of writings about Peacock by both contemporary and later commentators.

Stewart, J. I. M. *Thomas Love Peacock*. Writers and their Work Series. London: Longmans, Green & Co., 1963. A useful pamphlet-length assessment.

Van Doren, Carl. *The Life of Thomas Love Peacock*. London: J. M. Dent, 1911. The only biography to date. Useful for reference purposes.

3. Articles

Butler, Marilyn. "Myth and Mythmaking in the Shelley Circle." *ELH* 49 (1982):50–72. An important study of the use of myth in the poetry of Shelley and Peacock.

Chandler, Alice. "The Quarrel of the Ancients and the Moderns: Peacock and the Medieval Revival." *Bucknell Review* 13 (1965):39–50. A useful study of Peacock's medievalism.

Garside, Peter. "*Headlong Hall* Revisited." *Trivium* 14 (1979):107–26. Perceptive discussion of Peacock's first novel.

Hewitt, Douglas. "Entertaining Ideas: A Critique of Peacock's *Crotchet Castle.*" *Essays in Criticism* 20 (1970):200–12. Finds that Peacock fails to provide any satisfactory resolution of the intellectual tensions set up in the novel.

House, Humphrey. "The Works of Peacock." *Listener* 42 (8 December 1949):997–98. A brief but judicious assessment of Peacock as a satirist.

Joukovsky, Nicholas A. "Peacock's Sir Oran Haut-ton: Byron's Bear or Shelley's Ape?" *Keats-Shelley Journal* 29 (1980):173–90. A perceptive and informative account of a much-neglected novel.

Kennedy, William F. "Peacock's Economists: Some Mistaken Identities." *Nineteenth Century Fiction* 21 (1966):185–91. Identifies the various economists who appear in Peacock's fiction and corrects previous identifications.

Mulvihill, James. "Peacock's *Crotchet Castle:* Reconciling the Spirits of the Age." *Nineteenth-Century Literature* 38 (1983):253–70. Studies the novel's debates in terms of their historical context.

————. " 'The Four Ages of Poetry': Peacock and the Historical Method." *Keats-Shelley Journal* 33 (1984):130–47. Traces the influence of Enlightenment history on Peacock's most famous essay.

————. "Peacock and Perfectibility in *Headlong Hall.*" *CLIO* 13 (1984):227–46. A study of the intellectual background of Peacock's satire of progress.

Salz, Paulina June. "Peacock's Use of Music in his Novels." *Journal of English and Germanic Philology* 54 (1955):370–79. An interesting discussion of music as an ordering principle in Peacock's novels.

Spedding, James. "Tales by the Author of *Headlong Hall.*" *Edinburgh Review* 68 (1839):439–52. The best assessment of Peacock by a contemporary.

Index

"Ahrimanes," 6, 23–24, 35, 122
Antijacobin Review, 17, 51
Ariosto: *Orlando Furioso,* 86
Aristophanic Comedy, 86–87
Arnold, Matthew, 88, 124
Athenaeum, 10, 101, 109

Bage, Robert, 33; *Hermsprong,* 33–34; *Mount Henneth,* 33
Barth, John, 124
Bentham, Jeremy, 8, 9, 69
Bentley's Miscellany, 10, 118
biographical essays, 116–18
Blackwood's Magazine, 36, 59
Brett-Smith, H. F. B., 50
British Critic, 17, 47
Brougham, Henry, 88
Buffon de, George Louis Leclerc, 49
Burke, Edmund, 55, 56, 96, 105
Butler, Marilyn, 18, 23, 47, 69, 105, 108
Butler, Samuel, 66
Byron, George Gordon, Lord, 22, 59, 60, 62, 95, 97, 114, 117; *Childe Harold,* 26, 62; *Don Juan,* 26; *Manfred,* 26; *Vision of Judgement,* 24

Cambrian Quarterly Magazine, 101
Canning, George, 51, 105–6
capitalism, 39; *see also* commercialism
Catholicism, 85
Cervantes, 29, 112
"Chapelle and Bachaumont," 116
chivalry, 48, 49, 73, 113
Church of England, 85
"Clonar and Tlamin," 15
Cobbett, William, 115
Coleridge, Samuel Taylor, 24, 37, 50, 59, 65, 114; *The Ancient Mariner,* 50; "Christabel," 37, 63, 111; "Kubla Khan," 59; *Statesman's Manual,* 50

Collins, William, 12
comedy, 26–45, 59–68, 115–16; *see also* Aristophanic comedy commercialism, 70–80; *see also* capitalism
Compton-Burnett, Ivy, 30
conservatism, 51–52, 55–56, 65–68, 105–6; *see also* liberalism; Peacock, Thomas Love: literature and society, and politics; reform
cookery, 120
Critical Review, 15, 35
Croker, John Wilson, 51
Crotchet Castle, 2, 9, 29, 31, 32, 69–80, 100, 106, 107, 123

Dawson, Carl, 14, 33, 34, 115
Day, Thomas, 33
Denham, Sir John: *Cooper's Hill,* 16; *Windsor Forest,* 16
De Quincey, Thomas, 117
Dickens, Charles, 81
Diderot, Denis, 33
Dilettanti, The, 23, 35
Disraeli, Isaac, 33, 34; *Flim-Flams,* 34; *Vaurien,* 34
Douglas, Norman: *South Wind,* 124
Dryden, John, 33, 113
Drummond, Sir William, 23–24
Dyer, John, 12, 16; *Grongar Hill,* 16

East India Company, 1, 8–10, 69, 80, 118, 122
Eclectic Review, 20, 35
Edinburgh Review, 10, 36, 37, 118
enchanted garden, the, 82–84
Englefield House School, 3
Enlightenment, the, 27, 110
"Epicier, The," 115–16
Epicurianism, 82, 116
"Essay on Fashionable Literature," 29, 62, 93, 110, 111–12

Examiner, 10, 69, 110, 119

Ferguson, Adam, 39
Fielding, Henry, 29, 112
"Fiolfar, King of Norway," 15
Firbank, Ronald, 124
"Foldath in the Cavern of Moma," 15
"Four Ages of Poetry, The," 10, 12,
  27, 28, 108, 110, 112–15, 121
Fraser's Magazine, 10, 81, 84, 116,
  117, 120
"French Comic Romances," 30, 115–16
French Revolution, 51, 65, 96
Frye, Northrop, 34; *Anatomy of Criti-*
  cism, 34

"Gastronomy and Civilization," 120
Genius of the Thames, The, 4, 13, *15–*
  18, 20, 26–27, 28, 39, 52, 75
Gibbon, Edward, 2, 14
Gifford, William, 37, 51, 56
Gisborne, Maria, 8
Globe, 10, 119
Godwin, William, 7, 53, 60, 64;
  Mandeville, 62
Goethe, von, Johann Wolfgang, 64;
  The Sorrows of Werter, 64; *Stella,* 64,
  65
Grainger, James: *Ode to Solitude, Pal-*
  myra, and Tedmore, 14
Gryffydh, Jane (wife), 9, 10, 18, 19,
  69
Gryll Grange, 10, 29, *80–91,* 123

H. M. S. *Venerable,* 4
Hazlitt, William, 117
Headlong Hall, 7, 13, 26, 29, 31, 32,
  35–45, 46, 47, 49, 70, 75, 76, 81,
  100, 122
Hobsbawm, Eric, 97
Hogg, Thomas Jefferson, 5, 7, 39, 117
Holcroft, Thomas, 33
Holy Alliance, 97
Homer, 28, 120, 122; *Odyssey,* 82
Hookham, Edward, 4, 15, 18, 19, 27
Horace, 28
Horae Dramaticae, 116
House, Humphrey, 1

Hunt, Leigh, 46, 69
Huxley, Aldous, 124; *Brave New World,*
  124; *Chrome Yellow,* 124; *Eyeless in*
  Gaza, 124

Inchbald, Mrs., 33
India House, The. *See* East India Company
intoxication, 101–3
"Is History or Biography the More Improving Study?" 13

Jefferson, Thomas, 57, 118
"Jefferson's Memoirs," 119
Jeffrey, Francis, 37
Johnson, Samuel: "Life of Denham," 16

Kant, Emanuel, 114
Keats, John, 21, 117; *Endymion,* 20;
  Lamia, 20, 22
Kemble, Charles, 93
Kingsley, Charles, 85

La Belle Assemblee, 35
Lake Poets, the, 24, 53, 114
Lamb, Charles, 117, 118
landscape designing, 36, 41–43, 85
"Last Day of Windsor Forest, The,"
  118
L'Estrange, Thomas, 121
liberalism, 22–23, 69
Linnaeus, 49
Literary Chronicle, 93
Literary Gazette, 22, 58, 70, 93, 101
Literary Miscellany, 10
literature of engagement, 51–54, 108,
  112, 116, 123
local poetry, *See* topographical poetry
"London Bridge," 119
London Review, 10, 115, 116
Love, Thomas (grandfather), 2
Lucian, 33

Macpherson, James, 14–15
Maid Marian, 9, 29, 69, *92–100,* 101,
  104, 105, 111
Mallock, W. H., 123

Malthus, Thomas Robert, 47, 49, 55,
  56
Mandeville, Bernard, 38, 39; *Fable of
  the Bees,* 38
Manichaeanism, 60, 121–23
Marmontel, Jean Francois, 33
Melincourt, 2, 6, 7, 28, 29, 31, 33,
  46–57, 58, 59, 66, 70, 81, 84, 87,
  97, 98, 100, 105, 114, 115, 122,
  123
Melville, Herman, 34
"Memoirs of Percy Bysshe Shelley," 10,
  64, 84, 117–18
Menippean satire, 34; *see also* satire
Meredith, George, 10, 124; *Essay on
  Comedy,* 32, 124
Mill, James, 8, 9, 69, 80, 122
Mill, John Stuart, 8, 69, 84, 121
Mills, Howard, 66
Milton, John, 19; "Il Penseroso," 19
Misfortunes of Elphin, The, 9, 14, 29,
  69, 92, 94, *100–109,* 119
Mitford, Mary, 58
Monboddo, Lord, 23, 33, 39–40, 49
Monks of St. Mark, 4, 13, 23
Monthly Magazine, 47, 93, 101
Monthly Preceptor, or, Juvenile Library, 4,
  13
Monthly Review, 15, 17, 35, 58
Moore, Thomas: *The Epicurian,* 96, 116;
  Letters and Journals of Lord Byron, 116
music, 119–20

Napolean, 97
natural justice, 100
necessity, 44–45
New Republic, 123
"Newark Abbey," 25
Newman, John Henry, 85, 88, 89; *The
  Idea of a University,* 88
Newton, J. F., 5–6, 23, 39, 60
Nicolls, Edith (granddaughter), 2
Nightmare Abbey, 3, 7, 29, 32, 46, 47,
  57–68, 69, 70, 93, 111, 114, 123
novels of ideas, 29–30
novels of talk, 29–35, 80–81, 100,
  101
"Nugae," 14

Ollier's Literary Magazine, 10, 112
Opie, Amelia, 37
Orwell, George, 30
Ossian and Ossianic poetry, 14–15, 17,
  28, 92, 104
outlaw, the, in romantic literature, 97
Owen, Robert, 71, 78, 79; *Report to the
  County of New Lanark,* 79
Oxford Movement, 85

Palmyra and Other Poems, 4, *12–15,* 17,
  62
Paper Money Lyrics, 9–10, 24, 75
paper money system, 51
Pater, Walter, 124
paterfamilias, 78–80
Peacock, Margaret Love (daughter), 9
Peacock, Mary Ellen (daughter), 9, 10,
  80, 120
Peacock, Rosa Jane (daughter), 80
Peacock, Samuel (father), 2
Peacock, Sarah Love (mother), 2
Peacock, Thomas Love: aboard the *Venerable,* 4; characterizations of, 30–32;
  and "Charles" (a childhood friend), 3;
  childhood and youth, 2–4; as classi-
  cist, 4, 6–7, 20–21, 22; and cookery, 120; and the East India
  Company, 8–10; life of, 1; on literature and society, 110–16; as Mana-
  chaean, 121–23; and mother, 2–3;
  and music, 119–20; as novelist, 26;
  and poetry, 12–25, 27–29, 84–87,
  108–9, 112–15; and politics, 98,
  103–9; privacy of, 1, 116–17; and
  religion, 84–87; retirement of, 10–
  11; and romanticism, 5, 22, 114; as
  satirist, 1, 10–11, 27–29; and Shelley, 4–8, 20, 26, 46–47, 57–58,
  64, 117–18, 124–25; as student, 3–
  4

WORKS: ESSAYS AND REVIEWS
"Chapelle and Bachaumont," 116
"Epicier, The," 115–16
"Essay on Fashionable Literature,"
  29, 62, 93, 110, 111–12

"Four Ages of Poetry, The," 10, 12, 27, 28, 108, 110, 112–15, 121

"French Comic Romances," 30, 115–16

"Gastronomy and Civilization," 120

Horae Dramaticae, 116

"Is History of Biography the More Improving Study?" 13

"Jefferson's Memoirs," 119

"Last Day of Windsor Forest, The," 118

"London Bridge," 119

"Memoirs of Percy Bysshe Shelley," 10, 64, 84, 117–18

"Recollections of Childhood: the Abbey House," 118

WORKS: NOVELS AND PLAYS

Crotchet Castle, 2, 9, 29, 31, 32, 69–80, 100, 106, 107, 123

Dilettanti, The, 23, 35

Gryll Grange, 10, 29, 80–91, 123

Headlong Hall, 7, 13, 26, 29, 31, 32, 35–45, 46, 47, 49, 70, 75, 76, 81, 100, 122

Maid Marian, 9, 29, 69, 92–100, 101, 104, 105, 111

Melincourt, 2, 6, 7, 28, 29, 31, 33, 46–57, 58, 59, 66, 70, 81, 84, 87, 97, 98, 100, 105, 114, 115, 122, 123

Misfortunes of Elphin, The, 9, 14, 29, 69, 92, 94, 100–109, 119

Nightmare Abbey, 3, 7, 29, 32, 46, 47, 57–68, 69, 70, 93, 111, 114, 123

Round Table; or King Arthur's Feast, The, 23

Three Doctors, The, 23, 35, 41

WORKS: POETRY

"Ahrimanes," 6, 23–24, 35, 122

"Clonar and Tlamin," 15

"Fiolfar, King of Norway," 15

"Foldath in the Cavern of Moma," 15

Genius of the Thames, The, 4, 13, 15–18, 20, 26–27, 28, 39, 52, 75

Monks of St. Mark, 4, 13, 23

"Newark Abbey," 25

"Nugae," 14

Palmyra and Other Poems, 4, 12–15, 17, 62

Paper Money Lyrics, 9–10, 24, 75

Philosophy of Melancholy, The, 4, 13, 18–20, 23, 28, 62

Rhododaphne: or the Thessalian Spell, 7, 13, 20–23, 24, 26, 27

Sir Hornbook, 23

Sir Proteus: a Satirical Ballad, 24, 53

"Stanzas Written at Sea," 15

perfectibility of man. *See* progress

Philosophy of Melancholy, The, 4, 13, 18–20, 23, 28, 62

Plato, 33

Poetical Register, 15

political economy, 73–76, 77, 85, 101

Pope, Alexander, 16, 27, 113

Priestly, J. B., 5, 12, 32

progress, 38–41, 85–86, 103–9, 114

Pynchon, Thomas, 124

Quarterly Review, 36, 37, 55

Rabelais, Francois, 29, 32, 34, 112

"Recollections of Childhood: the Abbey House," 118

reform, 55, 56–57; *see also* liberalism

Reform Bill, the first, 81

religion, 84–87

Repton, Humphrey, 36, 41

Restoration, the, 28

Rhododaphne: or the Thessalian Spell, 7, 13, 20–23, 24, 26, 27

Ricardo, David, 75

Ritson, Joseph, 96

Robinson, Henry Crabb, 35

romanticism, 5, 47–51; *see also* Peacock, Thomas Love: and romanticism

Round Table; or King Arthur's Feast, The, 23

Rousseau, Jean Jacques, 40, 44

satire, 1, 27–28, 47–51; *see also* Menippean satire; Peacock, Thomas Love: as satirist

satiric romance, 92–109; *Satirist,* 17; *see also* satire

Saturday Review, 81, 84
science, 87–91
Scott, Sir Walter, 29, 48, 76, 92–93, 97, 114; *Ivanhoe,* 93
Scottish Enlightenment, 74–76
Seditious Meetings Bill, 52
Shaftsbury, Earl of, 33
Shakespeare, 93; *As You Like It,* 93, 99; *Much Ado about Nothing,* 93
Shelley, Harriet, 6, 7, 61, 117
Shelley, Mary (Godwin), 7, 61, 64, 65, 93, 117
Shelley, Percy Bysshe, 1, 4–8, 14, 16, 20, 22, 23, 25, 26, 32–33, 39, 40, 46–47, 48, 52, 53, 57–58, 60–61, 62, 64, 65, 69, 84, 93, 95, 96, 98, 117–18, 124–25; *Alastor,* 7; *Defence of Poetry,* 108, 112; *A Proposal for Putting Reform to the Vote,* 52; *Queen Mab,* 39, 40; *The Revolt of Islam (Laon and Cythna),* 7, 20, 23, 65
Sheridan, Richard Brinsley: *School for Scandal,* 64
Sir Hornbook, 23
Sir Proteus: a Satirical Ballad, 24, 53
Smith, Adam, 39, 75, 122; *The Wealth of Nations,* 76
Southey, Robert, 24, 32, 50, 55, 72, 95, 114; *Wat Tyler,* 95
Spedding, James, 121
Spiritualism, 86–87
"Stanzas Written at Sea," 15

Swift, Jonathan, 29, 112

Tennyson, Alfred Lord, 25, 81
Thompson, James, 12
Three Doctors, The, 23, 35, 41
topographical poetry, 16

utilitarianism, 8–9

Van Doren, Carl, 35
Vardarelli, Gaetano, 97
Voltaire, 29, 33, 34, 112, 120

Walker, George, 33
Wallis, Henry, 10
Warton, Joseph, 12, 27; *An Essay on the Genius and Writings of Pope,* 27
Warton, Thomas, 12, 27; *History of English Poetry,* 27
Waugh, Evelyn, 124
West Indian slavery, 47, 50
Westminster Review, 10, 69, 96, 116
Wicks, John Harris, 3
Wollstonecraft, Mary, 7, 64
Wood, Robert: *Ruins of Palmyra, otherwise Tedmore, in the desert,* 13–14
Woolf, Virginia, 1
Wordsworth, William, 16, 19, 50, 114; *The Borderers,* 97; *The Excursion,* 53; "Tintern Abbey," 16, 24

Zoroastrianism, 24–25

DATE DUE			

Mulvihill   208935